openGROUNDS

at the University of Virginia

Link . Learn . Lead . Live

Edited by Lindsey Hepler and William Sherman

OpenGrounds . Office of the Vice President for Research . University of Virginia

openGROUNDS

connect. collaborate. create | uva

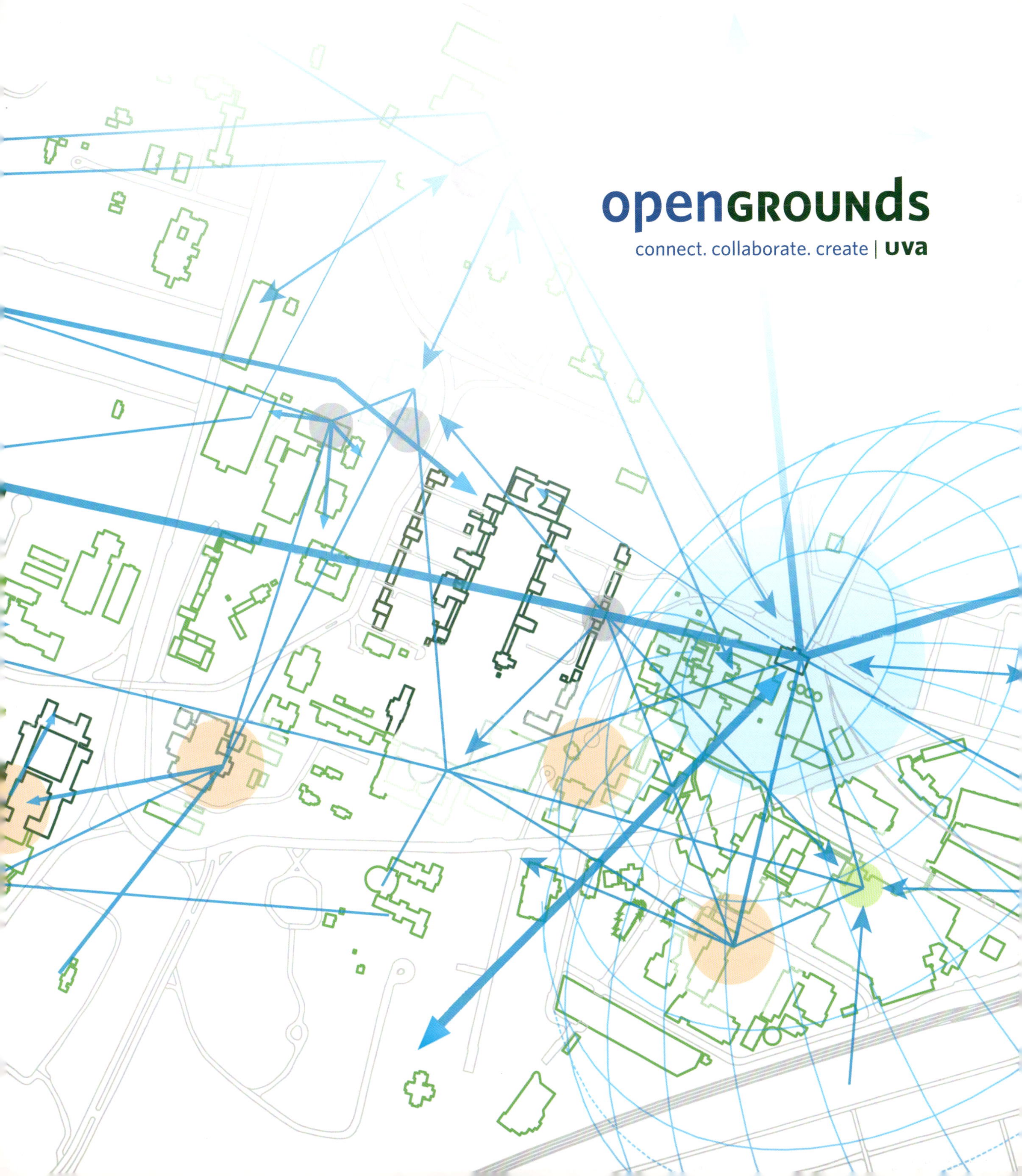

Philosophy and History

by
William Sherman
Founding Director, OpenGrounds, Associate Vice President for Research, and Professor of Architecture

The University of Virginia was founded as a revolutionary re-invention of higher education. Thomas Jefferson recognized the need for a different kind of institution that matched the tenets of the Age of Reason, where the search for knowledge would be unfettered by previous models of thought and institutional constraints. To meet the rapid transformations in contemporary research, scholarship, and practice, the university continues this tradition of reinvention with the creation of a new space, both physical and intellectual, for experimentation, risk taking, and boundary-crossing exploration. OpenGrounds carries forward the university's original spirit of innovation by creating new programs, places, and partnerships; catalyzing new approaches to important challenges; and inspiring new collaborations across and beyond the "Grounds." Since its launch in 2012, OpenGrounds has engaged students and faculty from all of the university's schools and disciplines to build both internal and external partnerships, between museums, governments, innovative corporations, scholars, and entrepreneurs. It has inspired new directions in research, performance, design, and public service, connecting unlikely collaborators and creative partners. Attracting national attention and inquiry from many quarters, OpenGrounds is a signal of the university's forward-looking vision and an engine to translate inspiring intentions into actions with impact.

opposite

Projects created by the Design Driven Manufacturing Architecture Studio, Fall 2014, led by Jeana Ripple, *Assistant Professor, Architecture*

below, left to right

The Entrance Building, built 1914
IMP Coronation, University of Virginia
Ralph W. Holsinger,
Courtesy of University of Virginia Library

The Corner Building, today

OpenGrounds is emerging at a time when the structures of knowledge that drove extraordinary leaps in understanding throughout the past 200 years are opening to a new set of possibilities. There is a growing recognition that contemporary global challenges have a complexity that will require a questioning of contemporary structures of knowledge that first emerged in the 19th century. Universities and many other societal institutions recognize the need for reinvention to support emerging innovation at the intersections of existing domains. While universities provide an unparalleled concentration of expertise and experience, with an equally unparalleled value to society, their capacity to engage beyond their boundaries must be enhanced and expanded. OpenGrounds was created in a spirit of institutional entrepreneurship to be a catalyst for this essential transformation.

Origins

OpenGrounds began in a collaborative design partnership sponsored by the Vice President for Research, which challenged faculty and students to imagine a hub for innovative research and creative work, where art and science could find common ground and the diverse richness of talent at the university could collaborate on those societal challenges most in need of fresh thinking. The students recognized that this was not about building a singular place, but creating a new network of spaces and activities that would weave into the daily life of the university community. Such a network would extend across and beyond the university, a lateral pathway through the schools and disciplines for the fluid sharing of insights. The underlying philosophy is to provide for a fertile cross-pollination of ideas to inspire new directions for research that will redefine the frontiers of knowledge. As many disciplines, professions, and organizations face the accelerating pace of change brought on by new technologies, this type of uniquely nimble test site is critical for the exploration of ideas without the constraints of pre-existing boundaries. At OpenGrounds, students, staff, and faculty discover new colleagues with widely varying backgrounds, people from both inside and outside the university who are wrestling with similar questions. Doctors work with architects on health challenges in Africa. Poets collaborate with musicians to find new forms of expression. Lawyers work with sociologists on impediments to democratization in North Africa. Innovative corporate executives challenge creative students to rethink social media and support healthier life choices. These represent just the tip of the hundreds of programs, gatherings, exhibits, and performances hosted or sponsored by OpenGrounds in its first two years.

Places

OpenGrounds represents a new type of space at the university. For both symbolic and practical reasons, a unique common ground was needed to promote a culture of open sharing. Fortunately, a space in the hundred-year-old "Entrance Building," the original University Bookstore, was available for renovation at an ideal location: on Main Street at the historic threshold between the university and the city. It would become a gathering place, the classroom of the future, where both the latest and the oldest technologies would be available to serve both intimate gatherings and public events. The space quickly proved to be an unexpected inspiration for those who entered; belonging to no one group within the institution, OpenGrounds is therefore a neutral territory for all. The architecture invites engagement—from writing on the walls to rearranging uniquely configured tables and interacting both physically and virtually through easy-to-use technologies that offer a full sensory immersion. The space does not remove itself from the outside world: Its entrance onto the street to the north and the reflection of changing daylight from the south serve to heighten awareness of its context. The innovative use of materials challenges expectations—concrete tables roll easily over the original wood floors while the technological infrastructure is gathered into sleek raceways that form both chair rails and a bookshelf. A gridded enclosure of recycled resin panels unfolds to reveal a flexible workspace, while a round-the-clock coffee bar invites a pause for refreshment and convivial gathering.

The design of the studio complements the design of the programs, materials, books, website, and virtual environment, all of which extend the mission well beyond the physical space. While design as a mode of thought and practice has emerged as a productive means to accelerate innovative research and scholarship in many fields, OpenGrounds brings design to the forefront of all its activities and communication. Each component is thoughtfully calibrated to promote connection and exchange, lower barriers to engagement, and inspire creative interaction.

Programs

OpenGrounds' programming is essential to the catalytic dimension of its mission, creating many pathways to become involved. Internal and external partnerships promote gatherings that multiply opportunities to discover intersecting passions. Challenges sponsored by corporate and institutional partners allow students to share their creative concepts and get personal feedback from practitioners, experts, and innovators. Vonage and Hearst Business Media launched a series of competitions intended to generate the best ideas on the future of social media, as well as ways to help people make better decisions about their health. Many entries came in from across the university, with participants ranging from undergraduates to post-docs. OpenGrounds partnered with the Presidential Precinct to conduct the national pilot for the State Department's "Diplomacy Lab," matching students and faculty with offices of the State Department to seek new approaches to difficult global challenges. A Fralin Museum exhibition of Ansel Adams photographs, lent by Lynn and Tom Meredith, was expanded to incorporate an exhibition and forum on contemporary photography and environmental action, a community-wide photography contest, a publication, and three student scholarships funded by the Jefferson Trust. Open Table conversations bring together university and community members to explore topics that are generated by faculty and student interest, including the health of cities, climate change, race relations in the university and Charlottesville, social entrepreneurship, and opportunities for engagement with visiting luminaries, ranging from John Holdren, the White House science advisor, to composer Philip Glass. Open Hours every afternoon and evening give students, staff, and faculty the opportunity to take advantage of the OpenGrounds studio for collaborative work, informal meetings, and idea sharing. Student interns promote a culture of engagement and interaction that yields a unique vibe. Each of the programs is designed to create an environment of open collaboration, with guidance available to translate the resultant directions and insights into strategies for action.

Impact

OpenGrounds has tapped into a need, felt both within and beyond the university community, for a place to work outside of conventional institutional structures. The interest in creating pathways for communication and experimentation across existing hierarchical structures is expanding exponentially. As OpenGrounds develops its physical space and virtual networks, it is also increasing the scope of its experiments, connecting the classroom to practice, and researchers to new collaborative partners. Its impact takes many forms—enhancing the student experience, enabling new partnerships, creating research opportunities, touching the lives of hundreds of students, faculty, staff, and collaborators. Many narratives emerge as we explore the way we learn, connect shared passions across boundaries, create opportunities for leadership, and model a way of living. This book examines these impacts and the specific stories contained within them, which reflect the way OpenGrounds has enabled partner organizations and programs to better fulfill their missions and individual people to realize their goals in unexpected ways. With initiatives exploring the intersections of art and science, photography and environmental action, frontiers of diplomacy and global challenges, human health and innovation in communication, OpenGrounds is not limited by pre-existing domains. It provides a forum to fulfill Thomas Jefferson's call to "follow truth wherever it may lead," pursuing open-ended questions without preordained outcomes. OpenGrounds invites the curious and the passionate to share in the creation of ways to realize their dreams.

The structure of this book—**Link . Learn . Lead . Live**—follows a cycle of continuous advancement, in which experience informs insight, research underpins leadership, and communication enriches the domain of possibilities. In each section, projects and programs that OpenGrounds has sponsored, supported, or partnered demonstrate the breadth and depth of opportunities for the application of new perceptions to expand the reach of the curious mind.

upper left

Philip Glass, *Composer*

upper right

Lindsey Hepler, *Associate Director, OpenGrounds,* with OpenGounds interns

middle

Philippe Cousteau, *Environmental advocate, educator and Partner, Azure Worldwide,* conducting Global Water Game/Chesapeake Bay Game

bottom left

The Young African Leadership Initiative Civic Leadership Institute

Impact

OpenGrounds has demonstrated that just a few people with a good idea can make a huge difference. A lean and nimble initiative, OpenGrounds has been able to leverage the resources of the university, the community, and our partners to create programs with great impact.

our impact

1.6

people administered OpenGrounds, assisted by 30 student interns, and in just

2.5

years, March 2012 to October 2014, produced dramatic results.

what we did

615

events were held, including sponsored programs, performances, flash seminars, workshops, retreats, OpenTables, receptions, and dinners.

$250,000

external funding was raised for programs, including prize money.

33

media appearances resulted from OpenGrounds programming.

who participated

750

faculty & staff who organized, hosted, and engaged in programming.

125

50 departments and **75 university organizations** were participants or contributors at OpenGrounds.

25

community organizations were involved.

who partnered

8

Alliance for Arts in Research Universities
Federal Executive Institute
Global Water Games
Hearst Business Media
The Phillips Collection
U.S. Department of State
Virginia Rural Health Association
Vonage

3

weeks from concept to national pilot launch for Diplomacy Lab, putting students in collaboration with US Department of State.

who benefited

4,494

people attended the OpenGrounds-initiated exhibition, *Ansel Adams: A Legacy*, setting an attendance record for The Fralin Museum of Art.

$83,000

in **prizes** and **scholarships** were disbursed.

36

universities and **institutions** have requested information about what OpenGrounds is doing and how they are achieving it.

Move forward!

A Day in the Life

Sample Day 1

8 - 11 Carter G. Woodson Institute postdoc bootcamp

11 - 12:15 Design Thinking class presentations

12:30 - 2 Open Table Discussion: The Thriving Cities Project

2 - 5 Open Hours

5 - 7 Flash Seminar: "Coffee Shops as an 'Intersection' and Doing Business as a Social Entrepreneur", led by Toan Nguyen, entrepreneur in the Charlottesville community

7 - 11:30 Open Hours

Sample Day 2

8:30 - 2 GABfest 2014: "Religion and the University," hosted by the Institute of the Humanities and Global Cultures' Graduate Advisory Board

2 - 5 Open Hours

5 - 7 "Drawing Attention" drawing workshop

7 - 9 *Technosonics* concert and panel discussion

VIRGINIA

GROUNDS
collaborate. create | uva
91.1FM

Creative encounters at Opengrounds build networks that connect diverse talent. Communication creates the potential for invention that lies beyond the imagination of the individual mind. Hierarchies are flattened as lateral connections eclipse the traditionally vertical structures of disciplines and institutions. The public responsibility of the university is realized in new partnerships and in the flow of ideas beyond the walls of the academy.

Link . Learn . Lead . Live

Opposite: Tom Skalak, *Vice President for Research*, and John Holdren, *White House science advisor*

Link

Public Day

Collaborative Events

Remarks by UVA President **Teresa A. Sullivan** at the inaugural Public Day event in April 2014.

Good evening. I'm UVA President Teresa Sullivan, and I'm delighted to be with you to help revive a UVA tradition that has lain dormant since it was discontinued about 150 years ago.

In the early years of the university, at the end of each academic year, top students would present their academic work and research findings to their teachers, classmates, and the general public at Public Day. This day was meant to be a showcase for student achievement. We are reviving Public Day in 2014 to serve the same purpose.

Our faculty and students work at the frontiers of discovery in every field. When you push the boundaries of a frontier, there is always risk involved. The student work you will hear about today is the result of courageous exploration and imagination.

> "Thomas Jefferson designed the University's Academical Village to encourage close collaboration and creativity among students and faculty members. OpenGrounds is a modern manifestation of Jefferson's founding principles, as it encourages collaborative, cross-disciplinary work across the University. OpenGrounds connects scholars, researchers, artists, and external partners in ways that will generate innovative results."
>
> — **Teresa A. Sullivan**, *President*

We encourage our students to do this kind of leading-edge, exploratory work. This commitment is reflected in our new strategic plan, the Cornerstone Plan. Strategies in the plan focus on providing high-impact educational experiences that deliver new levels of student engagement, including experiences with global impact.

About an hour ago, I participated in a ceremony to unveil a section of the Berlin Wall that will be on display at UVA, near Alderman Library, for the next year. The installation is a testament to the liberating power of democracy, and it will be a source of both learning and inspiration for our students, faculty, and staff, as well as community members. I hope it will motivate our students to explore the story of the Berlin Wall and perhaps to open new lines of research in this chapter of world history.

UVA students are already pursuing cutting-edge research and producing works of creative scholarship in a great variety of fields—medicine, the arts, computer technology, architectural design, and much more. Today's Public Day presentations, and the exhibits taking place over the next week, reflect this great variety. The topics range from an agribusiness education program for women in rural Tanzania to Chinese

Teresa A. Sullivan

architecture; from an after-school health-and-wellness program for local schoolchildren to a reminder system to improve hand-washing compliance among healthcare professionals and an engineering team's design for a suborbital flight vehicle.

Today's Public Day coincides with our Founder's Day. This is the day we celebrate the birthday of our university's founder, Thomas Jefferson. Mr. Jefferson set the bar high when he created this university. In his words, he urged us "to explore and to expose every subject susceptible of its contemplation."[1]

Considering the student work on display today and this coming week, I'm sure that Thomas Jefferson would be quite pleased with the range and quality of our students' inquiry.

On Public Day 2014, I congratulate our students, as well as our faculty and community members who act as their mentors and their partners. And finally, I thank all of you for coming this evening to hear from our students.

1 Thomas Jefferson to Antoine Louis Claude Destutt de Tracy, December 26, 1820

Lindsey Brinton
PhD canidate
Biomedical Engineering
School of Engineering/
School of Medicine

Catching Tumors by their Webs

Stromal Imaging for Early Diagnosis of Pancreatic Cancer

Lindsey Brinton was recognized for her research project on pancreatic cancer as well as for winning the People's Choice Award in the 2013 Universitas 21 International Three-Minute Thesis Competition. The three-minute thesis is an important tool for recognizing and breaking free of disciplinary jargon in order to share research with a broader audience. Brinton's research seeks to detect pancreatic tumors before they even develop. Because the pancreas is hidden behind other organs, it has not been possible for doctors to detect pancreatic tumors while they are still treatable. A web of tumor support cells surrounds pancreatic tumors. By exposing the cells surrounding a tumor to "keys," the tumor support cells can be detected because of their unique protein "locks," allowing doctors to "see" a tumor in its earliest stages.

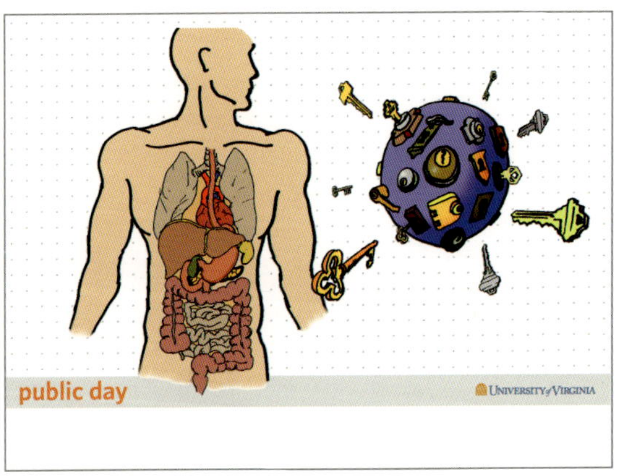

Asa Eslocker & **Harriett Jameson**
Master of Landscape Architecture candidates
School of Architecture

Landscapes of Longevity

Stories from the Uncharted Territory of Growing Old

Researchers for this project, awarded the University of Virginia's 2013 Howland Fellowship, explore public landscapes in three "Blue Zone" locations—vernacular landscapes whose inhabitants' daily work, food, and social routines enable them to live measurably longer, healthier lives and work well into old age. The three locations, all characterized by extreme longevity, are Loma Linda, California; the Ogliastra and Barbagia regions of Sardinia, Italy; and the Ogimi and Kunigami districts of Okinawa, Japan. In order to understand how public places can shape cultures of healthy aging, researchers used a cultural landscape perspective to examine how physical aspects of landscape can enable healthy communities, and how a sense of place can impact well-being. The findings are presented in a documentary film highlighting the qualitative connections between landscapes and longevity through personal narratives, rich descriptions, daily routines, and spatial practices. A greater understanding of Blue Zone landscapes can foster innovative insights and ideas for public spaces that will engender healthy aging in the United States.

Yekaterina Gilbo
Class of 2017
Physics major
College of Arts and Sciences

The Sun-Earth Connection

Earth's Magnetosphere and Solar Storms

Energy propagation from the sun to the earth through the magnetosphere determines our local environment, with critical implications for life and technology. The discovery of special magnetic frequencies detected in the magnetic bubble surrounding the earth (which protects it from solar radiation) has raised interesting questions about the role of space weather in our environment. Today, a network of satellites and ground magnetometers searches for correlations between solar wind and the earth's magnetic field. The results show that the correlation between solar density oscillations and magnetic field oscillations is strong, but more events must be identified and analyzed, both visually and statistically, to understand how solar activity changes earth's magnetic environment. This requires computerizing the identification process in order to gather enough events for statistical analysis, which is the ultimate goal. The idea that the sun directly oscillates the magnetic bubble surrounding earth has implications for the study of solar structure and turbulence and for understanding how energy is propagated through magnetic fields.

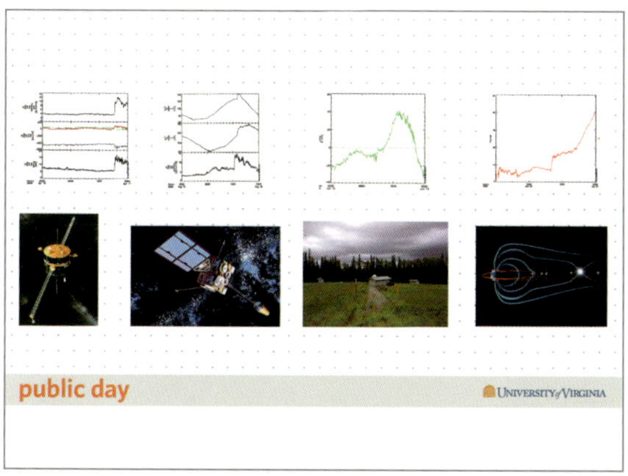

Alex Dumitriu, **Bailey Morton**,
Ilgiz Saubanov, & **Jen Casto**
Master of Public Policy candidates
Frank Batten School of
Leadership and Public Policy

C4C, Chitenges 4 Change

Empowering Women through Hygiene and Entrepreneurship

As a Peace Corps volunteer in Zambia, Jen Casto noticed that female students missed more classes than males. One girl admitted this was because they did not have sanitary pads. Jen made washable pads by hand with the girls; when women in her village heard about the pads, they ran out of stock within hours. After that, the girls attended school more regularly. Poor women miss up to 50 days of work every year because of their period. Many turn to unsanitary materials to make their own alternatives. When a woman cannot afford pads, her self-determination and health are compromised. C4C will partner with tailoring schools to produce the pads, and will sell them in bulk to NGOs, church groups, and microfinance institutions that employ women. Estimates indicate that a three-pack of pads will last a woman for one year. Materials are projected to cost $0.70/pack, with the consumer paying $1.50/pack. In the short term, C4C's pads will promote improved health and wellness outcomes for women, and will contribute to greater gender equity in the long term.

Winner of the UVA Entrepreneurship Cup

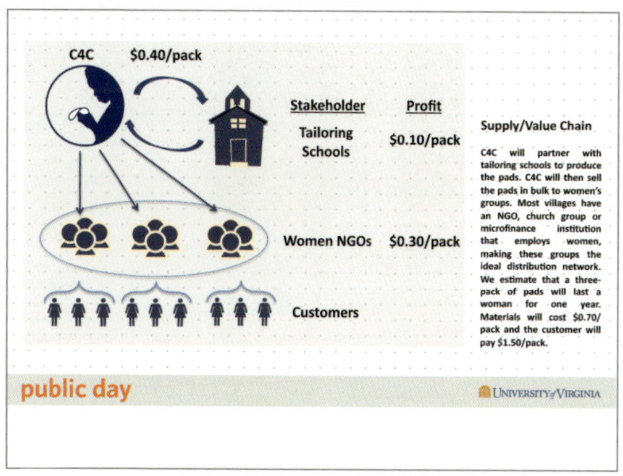

Open Hours
Student Perspectives

OpenGrounds Initiative

by

Sreemoyee Som
OpenGrounds student intern, Class of 2016, Biomedical Engineering major School of Engineering

The glass on the door emblazoned with the OpenGrounds logo squeaks below my persistent palm. By habit, my fingertips immediately curl around the doorknob to unlock the door. It is a Saturday morning and I am opening our Corner Studio to welcome innovative students, faculty, staff, and community members for Open Hours. As I walk to the light switches and soundboard to set the ambience for the day, I muse that these rhythmic actions ingrained into my role as an intern are a stark contrast to the unpredictable variety that every Open Hours is sure to bring.

> "During Open Hours, OpenGrounds is a space that frees me to flesh out my ideas, work through problems I'm facing, and pursue topics I'm curious about. The free coffee doesn't hurt, either!"
>
> — **Kaija Flood**, *OpenGrounds student intern, Class of 2015, Global Development Studies major*

No two Open Hours sound the same. On various weekday afternoons, I have entered the studio to the serious hum generated by a meeting of an interdisciplinary group of professors, or to the clamor of a lively student-led Flash Seminar on Kombucha production. On weeknights I have used the electronic beats of Alt-J to propel students into the early hours of the morning as we pored over ideas for the annual entrepreneurship competition, a project to create a new student-led clinic, or met the ever present demands of classwork. From experience, I can attest that weekend hours in the studio are especially capricious: The drone of a water pump from a student prototype for cleaning surgical instruments has harmonized with excited arguments over the next logical goal for a student team's start-up. The only constant, a staccato that punctuates the space, comes from the Keurig in the back, churning out cup after cup of coffee for our intellectually and literally thirsty visitors.

Open Hours is just what the name implies—an opportunity to use the OpenGrounds studio without the limiting constraints of pre-booking or having to focus on a specific meeting. Students, professors, and members of the broader Charlottesville community stroll through the double doors and end up spending more time in this haven of innovation than they had previously intended. A frequent Open Hours visitor and recent addition to the intern team, Kaija Flood has described the experience as liberating and caffeinating.

Word of mouth from previous visitors is responsible for bringing new acquaintances to our studio, but what is it about the Open Hours experience that draws students back day after day? The large touch-screen monitors and wall-to-wall whiteboards might be a contributing factor. But I'd like to think that the intern on duty, the maestro of each Open Hours experience, is crucial to bringing OpenGrounds to life. We create an impetus for visitors to acquaint themselves with others working alongside them, hoping that the initial introduction and polite smiles between keystrokes will turn into a conversation, a new contact, or a new project partner. We insidiously arrange the distinctive concrete tables into shapes that force different groups to work in close proximity, and we take music requests from visitors so everyone in the space can connect over a shared melodic experience.

> "I describe OpenGrounds less as a space and more as a resource. I think of OpenGrounds as an opportunity for students to become more invested in their interests while also exploring creative paths through collaborative, exciting interactions with other students and faculty."
>
> — **Ben DiNapoli**, *OpenGrounds student intern, Class of 2017, Architecture major*

Each night when I lock the studio door, I can reflect on a different Open Hours experience—and each brings a new appreciation of the minds and passions constituting our community and a renewed understanding of what the network of OpenGrounds visitors can accomplish through collaboration.

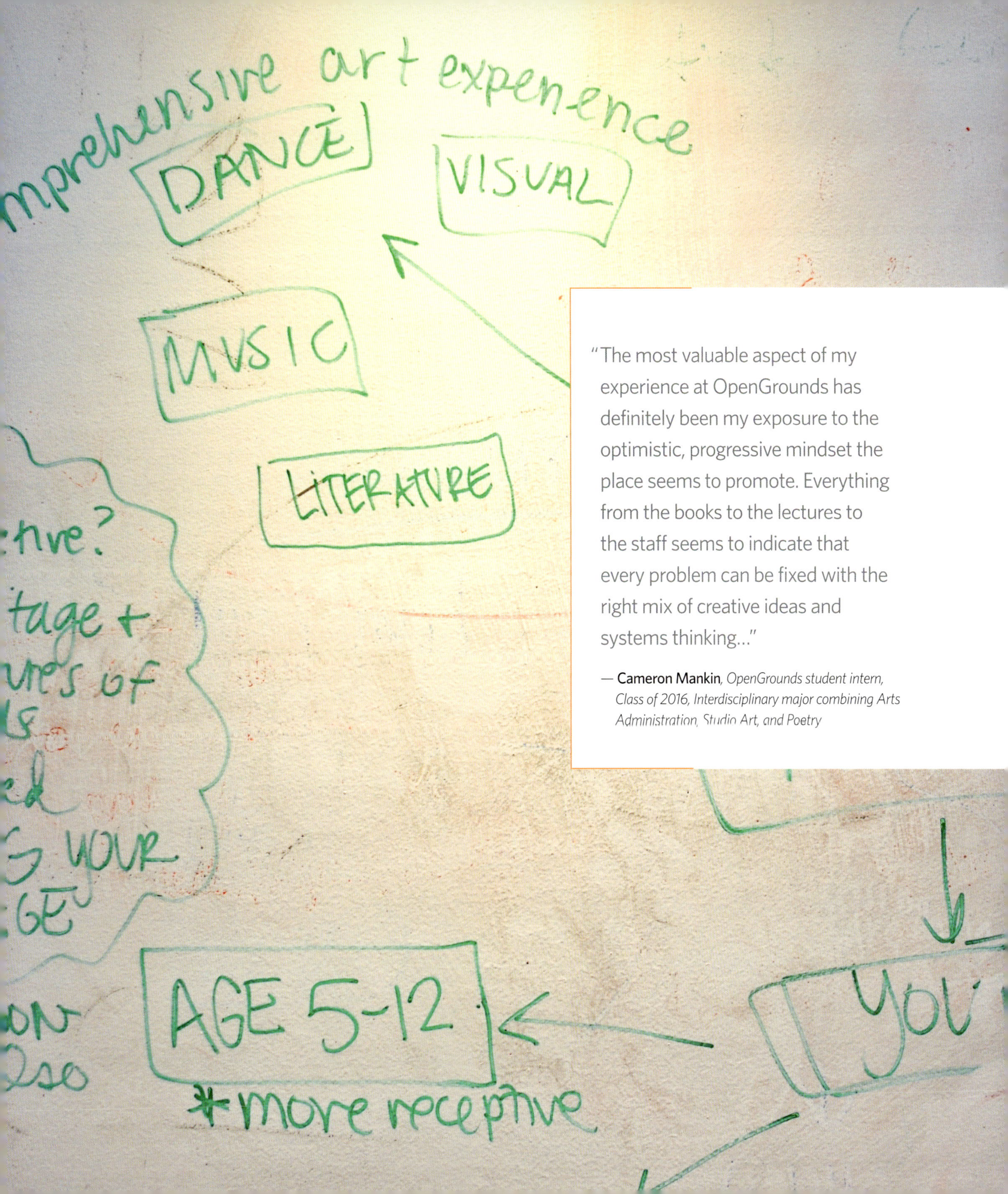

"The most valuable aspect of my experience at OpenGrounds has definitely been my exposure to the optimistic, progressive mindset the place seems to promote. Everything from the books to the lectures to the staff seems to indicate that every problem can be fixed with the right mix of creative ideas and systems thinking..."

— **Cameron Mankin**, *OpenGrounds student intern, Class of 2016, Interdisciplinary major combining Arts Administration, Studio Art, and Poetry*

Science and Art
An Ongoing Exploration with The Phillips Collection

OpenGrounds Partnership

by

Klaus Ottmann
Director of the Center for the Study of Modern Art and Curator at Large, The Phillips Collection

Museums are increasingly experiencing a shift from imparting authority (hierarchical education) to inspiring ownership (participatory learning). Today's museums require creative partners, like the University of Virginia's OpenGrounds, that inspire risk-taking, imaginative thinking, and belief in the life-enhancing power of art. Through the Center for the Study of Modern Art, The Phillips Collection's public intellectual interface, the museum has fostered opportunities for dialogue between our scholarly and diplomatic neighbors and the general public locally, nationally, and internationally. We have a broad range of academic partnerships with the George Washington University, Georgetown University, and the University of Virginia that aim to endue the public with personal yet profound experiences of art and create diverse, cross-disciplinary programs that engage new and global audiences in the areas of art, cultural diplomacy, and social well-being.

In 2010, The Phillips Collection and OpenGrounds embarked on a longstanding collaboration. In 2010 and 2011, we co-organized two highly experiential and dynamic Art & Innovation Design Gatherings, meant to set the stage for the birth of new ideas of social and economic significance; at The Phillips Collection in 2012, we presented the multi-local premiere of a telematic opera, *Auksalaq,* a piece composed by Matthew Burtner, the renowned American composer and UVA associate professor of composition and computer technologies; and in 2014, with the assistance of UVA's Contemplative Sciences Center, we developed The Phillips Collection's first contemplative audio tour.

opposite

upper row, left to right:
John Baugher, *Associate Director for Contemplative Learning, Contemplative Sciences Center, University of Virginia;* Dorothy Kosinski, Director, *The Phillips Collection*

middle row, left to right: Design Gathering event at The Phillips Collection; Peter Schjeldahl, *Art Critic for* The New Yorker, *writer*

lower row, left to right: Brooke Rosenblatt, *Head of Public Engagement, The Phillips Collection;* Design Gathering event at The Phillips Collection

connect. collaborate. create | uva
Vonage
www.vonage.com

Vonage Challenge
What is the Future of Social Messaging?

OpenGrounds Partnership

by

Marc Lefar

Vonage CEO

McIntire School of Commerce '85

Social messaging is still in its infancy, and the breadth and depth of new ideas and possibilities are limitless. The excitement around developing new applications and in seeing how far we can take social messaging was embodied by the first-ever student competition at the University of Virginia's OpenGrounds in the fall of 2012. Vonage was privileged to sponsor the competition and work with OpenGrounds, which fosters an environment for cross-functional ideas and creativity to stimulate disruptive thinking and innovation.

The mission of OpenGrounds is aligned with our mission at Vonage—to pioneer new frontiers and disrupt industries and conventional thinking to provide game-changing products and services.

The Vonage-OpenGrounds Future of Social Messaging Competition challenged students to develop new applications and services in social messaging and to imagine its future potential. We saw an exciting spectrum of ideas that addressed real-world problems and provided practical solutions. With the right mentoring and development, these innovations could potentially flourish.

Universities, in general, are natural breeding grounds for innovation because of their large concentration of expertise across multiple disciplines. Some of the most significant breakthroughs and disruptive ideas in history have come from students and academics from disparate fields joining forces, bringing multiple points of view to help solve problems. The OpenGrounds model has proved to be a powerful way to inspire new ideas and encourage forward thinking. It also integrates the best ideas from students in various areas of study with guidance from top-notch faculty members along with real-world experience from highly seasoned corporate executives.

OpenGrounds not only provides students with exposure to the business world, but it also allows opportunities for executives, like several of us at Vonage, to step out of the corporate environment and gain different perspectives from the next generation of entrepreneurs and strategic problem-solvers.

Vonage's partnership with OpenGrounds has been an excellent collaborative experience that exposed the company to innovative ideas from the next generation of inventors and entrepreneurs. We are proud to continue our work with the university on other programs that bring the business and academic worlds together and yield new insights for both students and executives. Our experience with OpenGrounds has also given us an opportunity to interact with future leaders, inspiring the type of entrepreneurial thinking that makes companies like Vonage possible and successful.

HOO
2010

Brent Baumgartner
Class of 2016
Computer Science major
School of Engineering and Applied Science

1st Place

Attendr

$15,000

A localized, persistent social messaging virtual-event space platform that facilitates information sharing between attendees at the same event, even if they do not have previously established social media relationships.

Damian Warshall
MBA canidate
Darden School of Business

2nd Place

Listen-In

$7,000

A location-centric information and social media aggregation service that connects users and businesses to comprehensive venue-relevant information based on geographic proximity.

Niklas Philipsen
Class of 2014, Systems Engineering major
Benjamin Terner
Class of 2014, Computer Science major

School of Engineering and Applied Science

Murali Varadaraj
Class of 2015
Commerce major
McIntire School of Commerce

vonage challenge

3rd Place (Tie)

Planr

$3,000

A social messaging platform for events, enabling users to seamlessly discover and organize dinners, concerts, movies, and other activities with friends.

3rd Place (Tie)

Sort

$3,000

A social media platform that conveniently and intelligently aggregates social media and extracts social views as they develop.

business media

Hearst Business Media Challenge
How Can We Help People Make Better Choices About Their Own Health?

OpenGrounds Partnership

by

Rich Malloch
President,
Hearst Business Media

The U.S. has tremendous challenges to overcome in health care and in the health of our population in general. We are interested in fostering innovative thinking for improving health and lowering costs.

Hearst, one of the largest multimedia companies in the world, is now as much an information company as a media company, with a significant set of information assets in the healthcare industry. The U.S. currently spends nearly one-fifth of its GDP on healthcare—that's growing faster than inflation, and many of us in this industry are wary that healthcare is growing at a rate that will freeze out other public investment, be it education, infrastructure, or defense. How can we change this? How can we make a difference? That's why Hearst is here at UVA, at OpenGrounds. What we really want to do here is inspire. Business is the concept of good, better, and best. Through this competition, we want to inspire you to dig deeper, to think harder, and to push yourselves to do more than just "good enough," because that's not going to win. We're looking for the best ideas and we really want you to push yourselves to do your best possible work.

Rich Malloch, President

Tom Skalak, Vice President for Research, University of Virginia

Kenneth A. Bronfin, senior managing director of Hearst Ventures

Ellen Koskinas, managing director of the Healthcare Venture Fund

Justin Graham, chief innovation officer for healthcare

Kathleen Lavelle, **Isabel Preciao** &
Eneique Cavalier
Classes of 2014 and 2015
School of Architecture

1st Place

TruFood

$15,000

An app that would provide detailed information about food at the point of sale.

Jacob Manley, **Benjamin Nowak** &
Kevin McVey
Classes of 2014 and 2015
College of Arts and Sciences,
Curry School of Education, School of
Engineering and Applied Science

2nd Place

Sportakus

$7,000

A role-playing game that puts the player in charge of the gladiator, Sportakus, and offers in-game rewards for meeting fitness goals.

Megan Watson, **Sydna Mundley**, **Todd Stovall** & **Chris Wallace**
Classes of 2014 and 2015
School of Architecture

Mary Kate Skalitsky
Class of 2017
College of Arts and Sciences
Katie Bailey
Class of 2015
School of Architecture

3rd Place

MyPlace
$3,000

An app that would provide holistic rankings of the health of a community based on nine different factors.

Runners-up

Offered paid summer internships with Hearst.

Mary Kate Skalitsky was recognized for her concept, **Playground Town**, a pedometer-based computer game. Katie Bailey was commended for her presentation skills as well as her idea, **The Water Gap**, which would help individuals monitor their water consumption and become more aware of water usage as a global health issue.

"What started as a spontaneous decision to submit a 'health-related' project turned into an invaluable learning experience and summer internship with the Hearst Health Innovation Lab that helped shape not only my interests but also my future career path. I learned first-hand about the importance of interdisciplinary work by combining my interests and studies, as well as the value of taking risks and tackling challenges. This opportunity helped me grow immensely as a student, person, and future employee as I continue preparing for the next stage in my life. I am grateful for all of the unexpected journeys that emerged as a result of the OpenGrounds experience."

— Katie Bailey, *Class of 2015, Urban and Environmental Planning and Spanish double major, Global Sustainability minor, School of Architecture*

An unexpected conversation with an unlikely colleague is the catalyst for new insight; a book recommended by the dean of a different school triggers a new line of reasoning. The open mind finds rewards in an encounter with the distilled experience of an accomplished leader. Discovery is fostered at the collaborative feast of an Open Table.

Link . **Learn** . Lead . Live

Learn

DIY Brainstorming
How to Generate Big Ideas Anytime, Anyplace

by

Chic Thompson

Founding Fellow, OpenGrounds

and

Batten Fellow, Darden School of Business, University of Virginia

Think back to the last time you were stuck and needed to brainstorm solutions to a challenge. Were you sitting in a classroom or a conference room with your colleagues eager to engage?

Probably not...you were staring at your computer alone with your arms crossed and teeth clenched.

Here are some creative strategies to help you conduct your own one-person brainstorm with some divergent thinking techniques to overcome your lack of diverse participants.

Step 1
Define your Challenge

> "If I had an hour to solve a problem, I'd spend 55 minutes defining the problem and 5 minutes thinking about solutions."
> — Albert Einstein

An effective definition of your challenge addresses only one problem at a time and does not assign a cause or blame for the problem in the definition.

Your definition should identify the "pain point" you are trying to solve. For example:

- Google provided a search engine that allowed people to find websites and explore the Internet without knowing the URL of every page.
- Netflix saved people the trouble of going to a video store and worrying about late fees.

Your definition should not imply a solution. Definitions are about the "what" and the "why" and not the "how." Adding an implied solution in your definition can converge your mind too soon and you might miss some divergent inspirations.

- To determine the **What**, start with the end in mind. Ask, what is the result that I want to see, feel and hear when my challenge is solved? Be specific with your vision.
- To determine the **Why**, find the urgency to solve your challenge. Ask, why do I want to achieve this result? Be passionate with your vision. Describe why you need to overcome the challenge's "pain points."
- Additional insights for your definition will come by asking what would happen if you do not find a solution to your challenge.

Your definition can be a couple sentences or a few paragraphs, but no longer than one page. Then give your definition a four-to-eight-word "action-driven" title, one long enough to be specific and short enough to force clarity.

Step 2
Take Five: Five Solutions in Five Minutes

Now it's time to ask the **How**. Ask, how am I going to achieve this result? Be bold with your solutions. Take five minutes and brainstorm until you have five possible solutions.

1. ______________________
2. ______________________
3. ______________________
4. ______________________
5. ______________________

This rapid-fire brainstorm is a great warm-up for your brain, and it loosens you up to look for more possible solutions.

Chic Thompson is the author of *What a Great Idea!* and *Yes, but...* For more creative insights, go to www.whatagreatidea.com

Step 3
Reframe your Challenge to Break Old Thought Patterns

Ask, what do I need to be more open-minded about seeing new possibilities?

1. ______________________
2. ______________________
3. ______________________

Ask, what are the negative "killer phrases" that can stifle my creativity and my ideas? Here are some examples:

1. It's not in the budget!
2. No one has ever done it that way!
3. If it ain't broke...don't fix it!

Overcoming these killer phrases will turn the creative tension into a jolt of energy to sustain your perseverance.

1. Let's do a prototype that won't cost much money.
2. Then I'll have a competitive advantage.
3. I've got to break it to remove the "pain point."

Ask, what is unique about your challenge that you have not seen in another situation? Identifying the unique features of your challenge can help you see the root cause of the problem and the seed of the solution that you need to grow.

1. ____________________
2. ____________________
3. ____________________

Ask, what is similar to your challenge? What analogy can give you insight and strategies to benchmark? How would another industry respond to your challenge? How would Apple, Zappos, Starbucks, NASCAR, or another country solve your challenge?

Step 4

See your Blind Spots by Visualizing the Opposite

Be crazy. Brainstorm solutions you would never suggest as possibilities.
Ask, what would I never do?

1. ____________________
2. ____________________
3. ____________________

Then ask, what if I actually did this "never" solution? What's right about the crazy "never" solution?

1. ____________________
2. ____________________
3. ____________________

Finally ask, what's the exact opposite of the way others are solving your challenge today?

1. ____________________
2. ____________________
3. ____________________

What if you actually did this opposite solution? Could there be a breakthrough idea here? If so, flip an opposite into an opportunity.

Step 5

Step 5
Evaluate your Solutions

Take your solutions and put them on the wall or lay them out on a table. Rearrange them, combine them, and add to them. Be careful not to group ideas that, when combined, hide the unique value of the individual solutions.

Create a bull's-eye diagram with "Must Do" at the center, "Ought to Do" as the next ring, and "Nice to Do" as the outer ring. Then sort your solutions into the three rings.

Step 6
Renovate While you Innovate

As you are creating your solutions to implement, it is vital for you to identify unsuccessful or inhibiting resources and policies that you must abandon in order to allow your ideas to be successful. Two questions to ask are:

- What should I **start** doing to allow my ideas to be successful?
- What should I **stop** doing to allow my ideas to be successful?

The energy released from abandoning unsuccessful resources and policies will give you the time to implement your solutions.

Step 7
Present your Ideas with Passion

Many people only think of one way to present their solution: a PowerPoint presentation with too many slides, too many words, and unreadable charts. Create at least two different presentations for your favorite solution and see what you can learn from the different approaches.

Suggested presentation formats:

- The one-minute elevator speech.
- The fifteen-minute stadium speech to your 10,000 cheering fans.
- The tweet strategy: Sell your idea in 140 characters.
- The napkin pitch: It's just what is on the napkin and the story you tell.
- The billboard strategy: Sell the idea on a highway billboard. What's your headline? What's your visual? What's your call to action? Remember that people are driving 65 mph past your sign.

Step 8
Smile

When you feel stuck...smile.
When you are selling your solution...smile.
When your ideas change the world...smile.

openGROUNDS

Open Table Discussions

Open Tables at the Corner Studio are a platform for informal discussion on topics generated by faculty and student interest. These events often provide an additional opportunity for engagement with visiting luminaries.

OpenGrounds works with faculty, students, and partner institutions across the university to generate questions for discussion. Visitors to the university gather around a table with students; community members join with academics to explore current issues. The Open Tables described below showcase the breadth and variety of these conversations.

An Open Table Conversation
Environmental Humanities Colloquium

Collaborative Events

organized by

Willis Jenkins
Associate Professor of Religion, Ethics, and Environment

While there are many faculty and graduate students conducting research on changing human-environment relations, often with implications for fields beyond their own, there is not currently an arena in which to share research and pursue its broader significance. This colloquium facilitated interaction between scholars in the humanities, social sciences, and natural sciences, in the hope of stimulating the development of a collaborative research network.

In a time of austerity and critical reflection on the endeavor of the humanities across higher education, initiatives in the environmental humanities are attracting attention for their potential to foster collaboration across universities and to incubate forms of transdisciplinary scholarship capable of interpreting rapid, global integration of human and environmental systems. Renewed engagements among natural sciences, social sciences, and the humanities are in turn raising critical questions about the methods and ideas that inform our inherited divisions of intellectual labor.

By considering major projects underway within the environmental humanities, this colloquium provided an initial platform for reflecting on methods and challenges of transdisciplinary projects and for catalyzing collaborations among university faculty and graduate students focused in some way on "the environment" as their object of study.

An Open Table Conversation
Transduction: A Pedagogical Experiment

OpenGrounds Hosted

organized by

Cassandra Fraser
Professor of Chemistry

Transduction refers to processes by which signals and energies are converted from one form to another through interactive media such as materials, devices, or biological and sociocultural systems. This concept calls for a dynamic systems approach across geographies, length scales, and time, and serves as a powerful framework for exploring present-day sustainability challenges, the digital-device revolution, and current advances in science, technology, creative arts, and design.

Transduction is an interdisciplinary pedagogical experiment working through and across networks, partnerships, and environments across Grounds and beyond. It involves guest lectures, interactive resources, and collaborative project teams, and serves to uncover the ways that we shape and are shaped by signals—chemical, biological, optical, mechanical, acoustic, electronic, social—in our surroundings, allowing us to explore their effects on learning, community, health, and well-being.

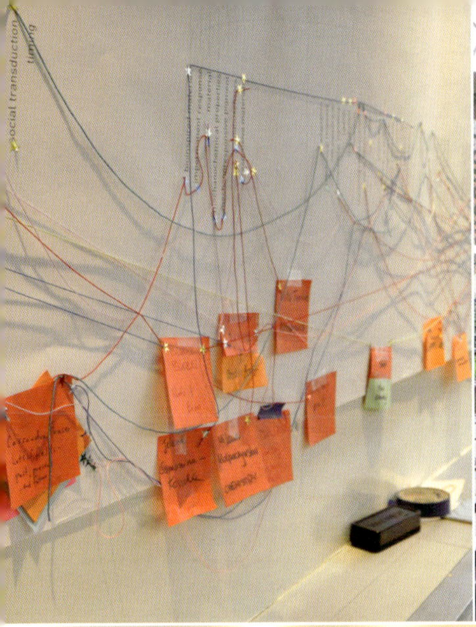

"As much as anything, Transduction was about learning how to talk to each other, effectively think and work together across disciplinary divides. It was about pooling our insights and expertise to discover, build, and illuminate connections. At the edge of understanding, students and faculty are on equal ground. Insights and good ideas can come from anywhere."

— **Cassandra Fraser**, *Professor of Chemistry*

HERNANDIACEAE
LAURACEAE
RUBIACEAE
ARECACEAE
PANDANACEAE

1

2

3

Transduction Guests Lecturers

Ram Eisenberg (1), an environmental designer/community organizer/educator/philosophical practitioner, told us about consideration, radical listening, and a community park project in Tel Aviv.

Jason Kelly Johnson (2), a designer/artist/technologist/innovator/futurist, stretched our minds with new approaches to teaching, maker spaces, and interactive public space and building designs.

Wilma Subra (3), a chemist/environmental health and justice policy expert/community educator/advocate, opened our eyes to health challenges faced by fence-line communities affected by petrochemical industries and fracking.

Tae Hong Park, a music technologist/composer/preservationist, outlined a new vision for computer music preservation and ways that urban sounds can be captured and transduced into visual maps.

Natalie Jeremijenko (opposite), an artist/scientist/engineer/environmental health activist, shared numerous projects turning urban environmental, health, and cross-species cohabitation challenges into interactive visual displays and convivial social gatherings.

Dorothy Parvaz, an Al Jazeera journalist/online editor/U.S., Middle East, and Japan political analyst, met with many groups while at UVA, sharing her harrowing experiences as a journalist and her perspectives on U.S. involvement in the Middle East, and urging greater awareness of media and the world.

An Open Table Conversation
Designing Online Learning Environments

OpenGrounds Hosted

organized by

Caner Uguz
PhD canidate
Curry School of Education

The Open Table series on Designing Online Learning Environments came at a time when online education was a large wave on the horizon that showed both promise and challenges for traditional institutions around the world. At the Curry School of Education, we were not only following developments but also conducting and contributing research on online learning environments. In the last five years we have observed a growing interest and increased activity in this field. While in the past companies such as Blackboard addressed existing needs for online education, the 2012–2013 academic year was characterized by a new momentum coming mainly from Silicon Valley, with recent organizations like Coursera and Udacity presenting fresh possibilities for online education.

There were certainly many voices and even small official and ad-hoc groups discussing these issues around the UVA Grounds. What seemed to be missing, however, was a conversation that addressed online learning not as an unstoppable force on the horizon but rather as an extension of a learning environment. We needed to step back and have a conversation about how online learning should be designed in the first place. The goal of this conversation was to understand what an online environment is and how the components of education, which go beyond instruction, could find their place within it. Education and technology professionals were key contributors, but discussions also required contributions from such knowledge domains as architecture, design, art, and engineering. This series of conversations—ranging in topic from education and space to the art and aesthetics of online learning, from creating community in online classrooms to online laboratory environments—represented collaborative thinking from the ground up about important principles and caveats in online learning from the perspectives of educators, designers, and practitioners.

openGROUNDS

Humanities in Place
A Collaboration with the Institute of the Humanities and Global Cultures

OpenGrounds Partnership

by

Michael Levenson
William B. Christian Professor of English; Director, Institute of the Humanities and Global Cultures

For a young Institute of the Humanities, still learning to toddle, no early encounter could have been happier than one with a slightly older sibling with a grand vision. OpenGrounds was an example and an inspiration from the start. But much more importantly, it became a partner. When I picture these last three years of our connection, as we siblings grew stronger, more practical, more ambitious and starry-eyed, it seems we were always running back and forth between Dawson's Row and The Corner. Either Bill was coming here for a meeting, or I was ambling over for another of his splendid events.

It's been the best of institutional ties, because it was always personal-institutional. Bill and Lindsey share rare gifts of temperament: no wonder they work so well together. They are clever and generous, eager to help, never gate-keepers but always Grounds-openers. Life at the Institute of the Humanities and Global Cultures would have been paler and much less interesting, and so would my life, if we hadn't had such partnership, such friendship.

At the center of it was the dream that woke me one morning and wouldn't let go all day, until by happy chance I met Bill on the Lawn. I blurted out, "I had a beautiful dream last night. I dreamt there was a Humanities Tent that stretched and covered us, hollowing a space where everything was pure, nothing compromised, where people talked about what mattered; where we recited poetry, and sang, and debated, and ate, and stayed up late, doing it all again." Then Bill said, "It doesn't have to be a dream."

So we began. We ordered poles and fabric; we gathered in a seminar with grads and undergrads. We read and stitched, sketched and reflected, did theory and practice, and made our tents and screens and mats. It all culminated in Humanities Week, the first of our two together, and now that it's just starting to recede—this collaboration in thinking and making, in the building of space and forging of community—it only glows more brightly.

No one was performing, no one claiming privilege or priority. It wasn't just the discovery of a possibility; it was a rediscovery, as if it all came back in a flash. This was what we dreamt of when we first imagined university life: reciprocity, creativity, frivolity, aspiration, comradeship.

In Spring 2013, the Institute of the Humanities and Global Cultures and OpenGrounds partnered to lead a series of discussions and a weekly seminar that explored, designed, and created a mobile, fabric event site, with deep cultural antecedents, to serve as a contemporary space for sharing insight. A work of architecture, literature, art, and science, the site created an engaging space used throughout Humanities Week.

Miller Arts Scholars
Facilitating Interdisciplinarity in the Arts

Collaborative Events

by

Cameron Mankin
Miller Arts Scholar and OpenGrounds intern, Class of 2016, Interdisciplinary major combining Arts Administration, Studio Art, and Poetry

The J. Sanford Miller Family Arts Scholars Program is an organization of diverse student artists who work to cultivate their own artistic talent through interdisciplinary discussion and collaborative work. The Miller Arts Scholars endeavor to have a meaningful presence in the art community while also facilitating dialogue and close relationships between students and faculty. For the first two years of the program's existence, weekly Miller Arts Scholars seminars were held in the OpenGrounds Corner Studio. As the Arts Scholars program grows, it continues to make use of the resources OpenGrounds has to offer.

In many ways, the Miller Arts Scholars are OpenGrounds' ideal audience—a group of independent, creative, interdisciplinary thinkers in need of an equally independent, creative, interdisciplinary environment. It was inevitable that the Miller Arts Scholars would become proponents of interdisciplinary collaboration. By the program's nature, it contains representatives from a variety of arts disciplines ranging from music to dance to drama to visual art. OpenGrounds provided a context in which to bring those disparate art forms into synergy. Through group discussions and, eventually, collaborative performance, we share knowledge and work to represent the arts. The Corner Studio even played host to our first annual Arts Scholars Showcase, the first display of its kind at the University of Virginia.

"OpenGrounds has an atmosphere that promotes forward thinking. The technology is modern and everywhere, but subtle. The dry-erase boards encourage collaboration. The light is natural and soothing, and the front windows open the space to the rest of UVA and Charlottesville."

— **Julia Pedrick,** *Miller Arts Scholar, Class of 2015, double major in Psychology and Studio Art*

OpenGrounds provided us with the opportunity to reach out and take advantage of the broad network of resources available at UVA for both artists and scholars. On numerous occasions a question would be raised in our seminar, only for that question to be answered by a professor who just happened to be working in the Corner Studio for unrelated reasons. Other times, connections made through OpenGrounds provided us with unique guest lecturers, visiting the university to attend another class, but more than willing to speak with our students.

From the government to the boardroom, a community gathering to an NGO in Africa, enlightened leadership is the key to the discovery of new paths. Leadership requires the capacity to listen, to act in the absence of perfect knowledge, to both seize opportunities and also recognize the time for restraint. True leaders thrive in complexity, perceiving the drivers of continuous change.

Link . Learn . **Lead** . Live

Lead

Designing Effective Organizations
From Jefferson's Academical Village to the 21st Century

OpenGrounds Initiative

A wide range of organizations including the Federal Executive Institute, Altria, the Weldon Cooper Center for Public Service, the U.S. Patent and Trademark Office, and many schools and universities have reached out to OpenGrounds to engage in a conversation about the importance of space for supporting dynamic collaboration.

"A truly *transformative* space creates a marriage between physical environment and institutional vision that fosters open inquiry and exploration and, ultimately, real change and expanded influence. Our individual and institutional capacities increasingly depend on access to what I call 'intelligence in new places.' This initiative—OpenGrounds—and the space they've created to support it have transformative implications not just for the University of Virginia, but for higher education and cultural institutions in general."
—Richard Koshalek, *Former Director, Hirshhorn Museum*

"One of the exciting things about OpenGrounds is that it's not just the students who stop by, it's also alumni like me. The concept of being 'open' is talked about a lot in Silicon Valley, where I'm from—innovation accelerates when you bring together people from multiple disciplines. The OpenGrounds initiative excites me because I'm interested in fostering innovation and outreach writ large. When I think 'OpenGrounds,' I think really open."
—Doug Garland, *Serial Entrepreneur; School of Engineering and Applied Sciences, BS '83, MS '87*

opposite

John Abele, *Co-Founder, Boston Scientific Corporation, founder of the Kingbridge Centre and Institute*

below left

Richard Koshalek, *Former Director, Hirshhorn Museum*

John Abele
openGROUNDS

Diplomacy Lab

OpenGrounds Partnership

The Diplomacy Lab, originally piloted by the University of Virginia and the College of William & Mary in Fall 2013, is an outgrowth of UVA's Presidential Precinct, a partnership among the University of Virginia; Morven; William & Mary; Monticello; James Madison's home, Montpelier; and James Monroe's Ash Lawn-Highland. The precinct, which is housed at Morven, draws on the democratic expertise of its partners to promote democracy. It has been host to numerous emerging world leaders, including members of President Obama's Young African Leaders Initiative

"The idea for Diplomacy Lab grew out of a simple question: What would happen if we could get America's best universities to help us solve some of the world's biggest challenges?

The State Department's 'to do' list is getting bigger and bigger, but our team is not. At the same time, America's colleges and universities are eager to reach out and engage beyond the classroom.

Diplomacy Lab allows offices across the State Department to identify issues that can benefit from additional research and innovation. Then, faculty-led teams at universities across the country focus on those issues over the course of a semester and work to develop new ideas and solutions. At the end of that process, we take their findings and channel them directly into the policy-making work that we do every day.

Diplomacy Lab is a great example of how we are reaching out beyond government to bring the American people into the world of foreign policy."

— **Tomicah Tilleman**, *Senior Advisor to the Secretary for Civil Society and Emerging Democracies*

"Open Grounds is the academic market place for UVA, where ideas flow freely across disciplines and every participant is both student and faculty. The Diplomacy Lab is an excellent example, where students have the opportunity to engage directly with real world problems with the State Department and to contribute to future solutions."

— **Stewart Gamage,** *Director of Morven Programs*

opposite left to right

Tomicah Tilleman,
Senior Advisor to the Secretary for Civil Society and Emerging Democracies

William Sherman,
Founding Director, OpenGrounds

Group Independent Project | Fall 2013

FACULTY ADVISOR: Gerard Alexander, *Associate Professor of Politics, College of Arts and Sciences*

AUTHORS: Daniel Rosenfeld, *Class of 2015, Double major in Political Philosophy, Policy and Law (PPL) and Philosophy,* and Schuyler (Sky) Miller, *Class of 2015, Honors Politics major, College of Arts and Sciences*

PROJECT **Rethinking the Community of Democracies**

BUREAU **Senior Advisor to the Secretary for Civil Society and Emerging Democracies**

Community of Democracies

A Report on the Implementation of the Design Model for the Community of Democracies

This report aims to assist the Community of Democracies (CD) in transitioning to the 21st century by improving its communication and innovation capabilities and providing institutional memory and organization. The implementation recommendations apply to the current CD structure. The implementation of the Design Model will create mechanisms for information sharing, support, and action by the CD and its members. The model will continue to shift the CD from a forum-based caucus to a more impact-focused force for the support of democracy and civil society around the world. In this report, we will propose five strategies to implement the Design Model for the Community of Democracies within its existing framework. Our recommendations are: 1) Solution Centers, 2) Social Media, 3) Regionality, 4) Capacity-Building and Training, and 5) the Consensus Decision-Making Model.

Development Economics | Fall 2013

FACULTY ADVISOR: Molly Lipscomb, *Assistant Professor of Public Policy and Economics, Frank Batten School of Leadership and Public Policy*

AUTHORS: Christopher Haberland, Yaqiong Huang, Natasha Reese, Samia Sekkarie, Yuanqing Zheng, *Candidates for Master of Public Policy, Frank Batten School of Leadership and Public Policy*

PROJECT **Women's Impact on the Informal Sector**

BUREAU **Office of Global Women's Issues**

Informal Sector Policies

Examples from Various Nations

We define the informal economy as including all economic activity that is not registered through the government. According to the International Labour Organization, the informal economy is often characterized as having the following lack of protections for workers: compulsory overtime or extra shifts; lay-offs without notice or compensation; unsafe working conditions; the absence of social benefits such as pensions, sick pay, and health insurance; and a lack of protection in the event of non-payment of wages. Some of the most critical challenges of the informal economy include not having access to training; limited access to finance and banking institutions; excessive government regulation; a lack of working premises, storage facilities, or toilets; low wages; lack of opportunities; and limited access to technology. This research examines policies targeting the informal economy in five countries: Thailand, India, South Africa, Nigeria, and Brazil. Our research indicates that countries are beginning to recognize the importance of the informal economy and are expanding initiatives to further support informal laborers.

> "I was fortunate to participate in both the Diplomacy Lab and an internship at the State Department with the same office. Over the course of the year, I was able to gain a deeper level of understanding of the work we were doing as my partner and I spent time interviewing State Department officials and NGO partners and reconciling their thoughts and ideas with relevant scholarship. In addition to honoring my research and interview skills, I learned how to write for a governmental audience (that is to say, succinctly) when we had to produce one discrete paper in which we made recommendations to the State Department office with which we partnered."
>
> — **Daniel Rosenfeld**, *Class of 2015, Double major in Political Philosophy, Policy and Law (PPL) and Philosophy,*

International Human Rights Law Clinic | Spring – Summer 2014

FACULTY ADVISORS: Deena Hurwitz, *Professor of Law, School of Law;* Aaron Presnall, *Lecturer, Department of Politics and President, Jefferson Institute*

AUTHORS: Patrick Dorsey, *Law '16;* Oliver Newman, *Law '16;* Liz Ramey, *Arts & Sciences '14;* Sam Shirazi, *Law '15;* Kaitlyn Tongalson, *Law '16;* Megan Wasson, *Law '16;* and Steve Williams, *Law '14*

PROJECT **Legal Reform Under Shariah Law**

BUREAU **International Narcotics & Law Enforcement Affairs**

Transnational Crime and Islamic Law

Overview and Recommendations for Legal Reform in Southeast Asia

The governments of Malaysia, Indonesia, and Brunei each have both secular and religious sources of legal authority. The United States and other members of the international community are active in combating transnational crime in Southeast Asia—especially human trafficking, drug trafficking, and money laundering. This report describes the mixed secular/Islamic legal systems in place in these three countries, analyzes the systems' implications for the fight against transnational crime, and offers several proposals for legal reform.... The civil and criminal law relating to our three transnational crimes remains primarily within the subject-matter jurisdiction of the secular courts.... Our analysis also reveals that the informal influences of Islamic law are perhaps the most important.... In short, the most challenging attributes of Islamic law to work with are not those cases in which an Islamic code controls particular conduct, but rather the areas in which Islamic thinking—or parallel Islamic authority—affects the actual execution of civil law. Managing transnational crime in these countries will require attending to these subtle interactions, on which we hope our research may have shed some measure of light.

Managing Sustainable Development | Spring 2014

FACULTY ADVISOR: Brad Brown, *Professor of Commerce and Management, McIntire School of Commerce*

CLASS: 32 undergraduate students

PROJECT **Food Security and Minimizing Postharvest Loss: Open Data and Innovation**

BUREAU **Economic & Business Affairs: Office of Agriculture & Biotechnology**

PROJECT OVERVIEW

Postharvest loss is collective food loss all along the food production chain, from harvest and handling, to storage and processing, to packing and transportation.... The State Department is looking for innovative ways to address postharvest loss challenges. In particular, our office would like to assess where technological interventions based on open data might lead to solutions to postharvest loss in developing countries. Given that postharvest-loss challenges vary significantly based upon a number of factors, students are encouraged to select a specific region and crop (example: India, pigeon pea).

STUDENT PROJECTS

1. Addressing Postharvest Cocoa Loss in Ghana
2. Postharvest Loss: Potatoes in Bangladesh
3. Postharvest Loss in Honduran Coffee

PROJECT **AMP (Accelerating Market-driven Partnerships): Scaling Impact of Cost-effective and Energy-efficient Initiatives**

BUREAU **Office of Global Partnership Initiatives**

PROJECT OVERVIEW

The project team will analyze and develop a business strategy for AMP's 2014 work. The planning process should be systematic and will include determining and refining mission, vision, and values; strategic goals; strategic analysis; and strategy formulation. The final product will shape AMP's work in the coming year and will be essential in helping AMP achieve its goal of developing, investing in, and scaling innovations that generate revenue opportunities, strengthen communities, and protect the environment.

STUDENT PROJECTS

1. Managing Sustainable Development: AMP Brazil
2. Avani Bio Energy: AMP India
3. Case Study: Chromium mine in South Africa builds world's largest solar PV-diesel hybrid power system
4. Composting in India

Student Leadership

OpenGrounds Partnership

From the beginning, student input and initiative have been critical parts of shaping OpenGrounds into what it has become. Student leaders from across the university have flocked to OpenGrounds to take advantage of its unique space and resources; and the OpenGrounds approach has in turn shaped these leaders into more open and creative thinkers.

Student-initiated Flash Seminars are one-time mini-classes that bring together faculty, students, and community members in small, informal settings to explore ideas and issues outside the formal classroom. Seminars are announced a week in advance and held in locations around the University of Virginia and the surrounding Charlottesville area, including the OpenGrounds Corner Studio, which has become an important resource for the Flash Seminar student team.

. . . . .

"I hope that most of all, OpenGrounds inspires a bit of rebellion in UVA students. I would love for students to begin thinking about the world they live in and how they can change it. I hope OpenGrounds breaks students away from the daily grind of assignments, exams, and deadlines and allows them to start thinking about how they can use their skills, and the skills of others, to think critically and create something wonderful."

—Agnes Pyrchla, *OpenGrounds Student Advisory group participant, Class of 2012, Commerce major, McIntire School of Commerce*

. . . . .

"My OpenGrounds experiences got me thinking even more about the serendipitous nature of creativity and inspired me to study the topic through my thesis research, connecting the dots between imagination, creativity, and innovation.

I met folks in the social entrepreneurship field through a Flash Seminar at OpenGrounds led by Toan Nguyen, an entrepreneur in the Charlottesville community, and was able to interview these people for my thesis. They were interested in using OpenGrounds as a resource to reach out to the university population, so I was glad to do my bit to help them in return."

—Manya Cherabuddi, *OpenGrounds Intern, Class of 2013, Commerce and Arts Administration major, McIntire School of Commerce*

. . . . .

Schuyler (Sky) Miller
Class of 2015
Honors Politics Major
College of Arts and Sciences

Student Spotlight

Throughout my time at the University of Virginia, I have been astonished by the unending range of passions, projects, and paths pursued by my classmates, faculty members, and members of the University community. However, even as I rejoiced in this wide array of disciplines and extracurricular opportunities, I became equally frustrated that the University in general, and my classmates in particular, often did not actively collaborate and interact with these different elements in order to challenge and encourage each other. During my second year, I began exploring ways to foster a more collaborative and engaged culture; specifically, I sought practical ways for members of the University to cross paths and not only learn from each other, but also work with one another. I believed that my peers, with their diverse research projects, knowledge, and opinions, deserved a space, a network, and a forum to engage in this purpose. It was with this in my background that I stumbled upon OpenGrounds. I was immediately drawn to its mission to create and perpetuate a culture of collaboration, connection, and innovation at the University and in Charlottesville. I had found a resource—both a space and a group of people—with which to work toward the goal of collaboration.

My first initiative through OpenGrounds was the Student Council program, Hoos Connecting, which brought together political leaders from across the University and the political spectrum to discuss relevant political questions. During my second year, I started the Democracy Network, a non-partisan organization dedicated to building a network of citizens committed to strengthening democracy collectively through collaboration and education. The OpenGrounds staff worked with me, connecting me to the right resources to start the organization and providing a space and technology for meetings. During my third year, yet another opportunity was made available to me through the OpenGrounds network: the Diplomacy Lab initiative with the State Department. I served as a student researcher and consultant for the Office of the Senior Advisor to the Secretary for Civil Society and Emerging Democracies, and through our work, my partner and I earned an internship with the State Department in the summer of 2014. Not only has OpenGrounds provided me opportunities for collaboration and innovation, it has advanced this culture across Grounds, with a physical space and network of individuals committed to its mission.

"OpenGrounds has hosted concerts, videoconferences, visiting scholars, graduate student entrepreneurs, the CEO of Vonage, the Poet Laureate, undergraduate classes, and more.

As an intern, I felt encouraged to think about the possibilities, but OpenGrounds invites all students to do the same. Do you want to start a documentary film club? Learn how to create apps? Teach courses on design thinking? Curate an art show? Well, you can. OpenGrounds is fully equipped and waiting."

— **Amy Curtis**, *OpenGrounds Intern, Class of 2013, History major, College of Arts and Sciences, Urban and Environmental Planning minor, School of Architecture*

Nick Lee
Class of 2015
Biochemistry major
College of Arts and Sciences

Student Spotlight

I first came to OpenGrounds at the invitation of the 21 Society based on my leadership within the Honor System, and my work with the Undergraduate Research Network (URN) soon led me back. I was organizing a networking event, aimed to connect undergraduates from different disciplines, and I was unsure of the next steps to take. Through a conversation with the leaders of OpenGrounds, I learned how to design an event that revolved around gauging the passions and interests of the students who would be attending. This approach allowed us to draw on the energy coming from the participants themselves, and ensured a successful event that brought together writers, environmental scientists, and engineers to contemplate what the biggest problems confronting society were, and how to face them. It was the first time an interdisciplinary event such as this had taken place at the undergraduate level. But perhaps more importantly, this experience began to shape my leadership philosophy.

In my roles as a student leader, I advocate for OpenGrounds and help expose other students to its space and philosophy as early as possible. For example, I worked with the Office of the Dean of Students to ensure that OpenGrounds had a place at Leadership 2000, a program where approximately thirty-five of the University's student leaders work and collaborate over a six-day period. By introducing future student leaders to OpenGrounds, we hope that they will take advantage of the collaborative environment and, remembering the founding philosophy of OpenGrounds, work together across organizational boundaries to achieve true university-wide initiatives with the full support of the student body.

OpenGrounds is supporting a new generation of leaders through its philosophy of interdisciplinary collaboration, not only across fields, but through a diverse network that increases the level of institutional memory as older, experienced students pass down their knowledge to future leaders. As these students graduate and move into the community, OpenGrounds will be an irreplaceable catalyst in fostering leadership in new students, who will go on to tackle societal challenges of the upcoming decades.

We measure success by the quality of life we enable for the greatest number—recorded in the health of our bodies, cities, and global habitat. We ask the hard questions in many forms to challenge priorities and imagine better alternatives. Artists and scientists, working on the same issues with rigor and creativity, find a shared language to extend their capacity for innovation.

Link . Learn . Lead . **Live**

Live

Changing Views
Photography and Environmental Action

OpenGrounds Initiative

"Changing Views: Photography and Environmental Action" was a series of programs and events surrounding The Fralin Museum of Art 2013 exhibitions, *Ansel Adams: A Legacy* and *Looking at the New West: Contemporary Landscape Photography.*

OpenGrounds is deeply indebted to Lynn and Tom Meredith, lenders of the storied collection of Ansel Adams photographs that served as the catalyst for a series of programs exploring the relationship between photography and environmental conservation, including two photography exhibits at The Fralin Museum of Art, an OpenGrounds forum and publication, a photography challenge, and student scholarships. This incredible collection of Adams's images, gathered by the Friends of Photography under Adams's leadership, has given us the opportunity to reach into the university, the community, and beyond.

These programs were made possible through the generous support of the Jefferson Trust, an initiative of the UVA Alumni Association; the PBR Lecture Series at UVA; The Fralin Museum of Art; the Office of the Vice President for Research; and Lynn and Tom Meredith.

Mike Osborne
American, b. 1978
Vertellus (Peak), 2012
Courtesy of the artist and
Holly Johnson Gallery, Dallas
Originally commissioned and
produced by Artpace San Antonio.

Ansel Adams
American, 1902–1984
Winter Sunrise, Sierra Nevada, from Lone Pine, California, 1944

Jon Bellona

PhD candidate in Composition
and Computer Technologies
Music Department
College and Graduate School
of Arts and Sciences

The OpenGrounds Art and Environmental Action Student Scholars Program represents the culmination of the "Changing Views: Photography and Environmental Action" project. These scholarships served as the pilot of the OpenGrounds Student Scholars Program and provided funding for four exceptional students, pursuing three projects and working with faculty mentors, to develop and implement new ideas at the intersection of art, research, and scholarship.

#CarbonFeed

With the advent of social media like Facebook, Twitter, and Instagram, humans have increased their production of digital content. Even simple online interactions generate carbon emissions; a Google search has been estimated to generate a minimum of 0.2 grams of CO_2e. To keep pace with growing online media, there is an increasing dependence upon data centers, which now account for almost two percent of the world's electricity consumption.

#CarbonFeed challenges the popular notion that virtuality is disconnected from reality. Through sonifying Twitter feeds and correlating individual tweets with data visualizations in public spaces, the work hopes to reveal the environmental cost of online behavior and its supportive physical infrastructure. Specifically, the project will map carbon emission equivalents from tweets in order to demonstrate the varying degrees in which we experience social media as pollutant.

#CarbonFeed occurred throughout the month of September 2014 in various libraries across UVA Grounds. By utilizing spaces that disseminate media, the project's hope was to holistically engage all sectors of the UVA community. #CarbonFeed is supported in part by a project website, carbonfeed.org

Gwendolyn McGinn & **Rachel Vassar**
Master of Landscape Architecture candidates
School of Architecture

The Infrastructural Wild

Abandoned infrastructure litters the American landscape, and for many people these spaces are devoid of meaning or, worse, held in disdain. Where the casual viewer sees nothing, industrious "weeds" put down roots and introduce ecological abundance to forgotten lands. By highlighting the unseen forces at work in landscapes of the margins, our project will reveal the chasm between the anthropocentric perception of absence and the reality of spaces full of species diversity and temporal variation.

Focusing on three sites in Virginia that are representative of three typologies of abandoned transportation infrastructure—canal, railroad, and roadway—we will show how each site is shaped by the spatial and material requirements of its original use, and how, after being decommissioned, each site intersects with complex systems over time. A series of hybrid drawings documenting these sites will be curated into a field guide, which will contribute to a greater understanding of the ecological, chemical, and temporal forces at play. These sites serve as examples of the neglected spaces found throughout the United States. Their study will increase the viewer's appreciation of his or her own local urban wilds, in terms of their ability to create habitat and the melancholy beauty they occasion.

Erik Deluca
PhD candidate in Composition and Computer Technologies
Music Department
College and Graduate School of Arts and Sciences

Community Listening in Isle Royale National Park

Community Listening in Isle Royale National Park traces the dialogue between a composer, a team of wolf biologists, and a community of park explorers who share a unique, deep listening relationship. The scientists involved in this project are the primary investigators in the five-decade-long wolf/moose project, the longest continuous wildlife study in the world. These researchers determine clues of wolf reproduction by listening for the sounds of group howling during the summer months, when excitement at den sites erupts during pup feeding time. For these clues, the researchers' ears, or "antennas" as they put it, tap into a network of visitors and employees who are scattered across the island, listening. This listening network is directly tied to the ecological well-being of the park, which is currently at risk of major change because the wolves, who play a vital role in the park's ecosystem, are on the brink of "blinking out" due to global climate change.

The project resulted in an ethnographic composition meant to create a space for self-perusal and discovery. It weaves together several different types of sound data collected during fieldwork: soundscape recordings of the place, interviews with researchers, interviews with park visitors and employees, audio diaries, an audio essay derived from field notes, and archival recordings.

studio reCOVER 2012

Center for Global Health

Collaborative Events

The unique relationship between the University of Virginia Center for Global Health and OpenGrounds begins with their co-location, next door to each other in the Corner Building on Main Street, and extends into their complementary missions to address critical challenges through new types of collaboration between the university and global partners.

"The field of global health is rapidly evolving. Partners from varied backgrounds and perspectives bring great talents that increase the likelihood of unforeseen possibility in interventions and collaborations. Even as new and old issues continue to demand moral, intelligent, innovative responses, we are realizing that, in an increasingly globalized world, these issues are often shared. Global is local."

— **Rebecca Dillingham**, *Director, Center for Global Health, Assistant Professor of Medicine, Division of Infectious Diseases and International Health*

UVA Global Health Case Competition

The UVA Global Health Case Competition aims not only to create a space for interdisciplinary collaboration, but also to inspire innovation in addressing complex and relevant global health issues. Answers are never "Googleable," and the most successful proposals come from a combination of diverse perspectives. To encourage this plurality of thought, the first competition required all 16 teams to have at least three different disciplines represented among their members. The case itself was also written by an interdisciplinary team, including engineering, public policy, international relations, and medical school students. By the time the teams presented their recommendations to judges on competition day, they had wrestled with the case for four days and vetted ideas with UVA faculty and graduate student mentors with topical insight.

OpenGrounds provided working space both in the days leading up to the competition and during the week of the competition itself. Intrigued by the dual prospects of competition and collaboration in global health, students came to OpenGrounds to learn about this opportunity in late January and returned during competition week for team brainstorming sessions, a midweek Open Table discussion, and the chance to grab food and relax the night before the event's final day. In the months leading up to the competition, the student case writers met at the OpenGrounds Corner Studio as they explored ideas, vetted information, and developed a well-researched, challenging case.

— **Colleen Laurence**, *Center for Global Health Student Liaison and Research Coordinator*

Rwanda Arts Collaborative

The Rwanda Arts Collaborative evolved from connections formed by Art with a Mission—Charlottesville, Art with a Mission—Rwanda, the University of Virginia Global Surgery Initiative, and the UVA Center for Global Health. The association of diverse organizations provided a strong network of support for shared priorities: a focus on the health and well-being of children globally, equitable interdisciplinary collaboration among international partners, opportunities for university student scholars to learn and contribute in a global context, and the potential for the arts to promote human health.

With its multimedia environment, the OpenGrounds Corner Studio supports and facilitates collaboration among the disciplines, diminishes obstacles associated with time and geographic differences, and invites diversity of perspective. It provided a remarkable environment for the Rwanda Arts Collaborative events in Fall 2013, serving as the university site for an exhibit of paintings created by Rwandan children and hosting a talk by a highly esteemed guest of the university, Professor Patrick Kyamanywa, Associate Professor of General Surgery and Dean, Faculty of Medicine, National University of Rwanda. Speaking to an audience of UVA students and faculty who shared his deep commitment to global health, Professor Kyamanywa addressed the critical need for direct connections and the value of working in another culture. The virtual participation of artists, students, and children both in the local community and in Rwanda spoke to the remarkable opportunity for collaboration provided by OpenGrounds.

— **April Ballard**, *Associate Director of Program Development, Center for Global Health*

1, 3
Rwanda Arts Collaborative

2
The Corner Studio

4-6
Water and Health in Limpopo (WHIL) research collaboration

2

3

1

4

5

6

Chapter 1
EXIT
tinfoil placed on cymbal

OpenGrounds as Media Garage

Collaborative Events

"OpenGrounds is an important tool for my research at UVA. For projects such as *Auksalaq,* the ZeroSpace Conference on Distance and Interaction, NOMADS (Network-Operational Mobile Applied Digital System) and *Technosonics,* it functions as a kind of media 'garage,' a place where we can test prototypes, workshop ideas, and present tech-heavy small events using immersive audiovisual diffusion. A 21st-century composer wears lots of hats. Like Beethoven, Brahms, Bartók, and all composers of the past, we still need to sit alone for hours in a world of sound, pulling sonic ideas from the imagination and turning them around like clay, designing melodies, rhythms, timbres, and forms. Most of us get into composing for the joy of this part of the job, the physical expression of ideas in sound. But to realize a large-scale project like *Auksalaq* requires extensive collaborations with teams of people. A composer might need to program original software or engineer a new hardware instrument, conduct field research, raise funds, produce and direct events, design graphics, and launch a publicity campaign, among other tangential activities. I easily spent as much time on these as on the actual compositional work. I was part of about five teams working simultaneously on different parts of *Auksalaq.* I composed the music and libretto alone, but everything else was created in collaboration."

— **Matthew Burtner**, Associate Professor of Music

. . . . .

Auksalaq, a telematic opera, was composed by UVA associate music professor Matthew Burtner and media artist Scott Deal, and involved performers and audience members in the District of Columbia, Norway, Montreal, Alaska, New York City, Charlottesville, and Indianapolis. During performance, the stages were connected through advanced telematic technology, allowing performers to collaborate via the Internet in real time.

Following a postponement due to Hurricane Sandy, which forced two of the scheduled seven worldwide venues to cancel the premier performance of *Auksalaq,* The Phillips Collection in Washington, D.C., the Lu Magnus Gallery in New York City, and the University of Virginia/OpenGrounds in Charlottesville, Virginia, hosted the U.S. East Coast reprise of the award-winning telematic opera, *Auksalaq.*

below

Detail of Matthew Burtner's score for *Auksalaq*
© Matthew Burtner, 2012, BMI

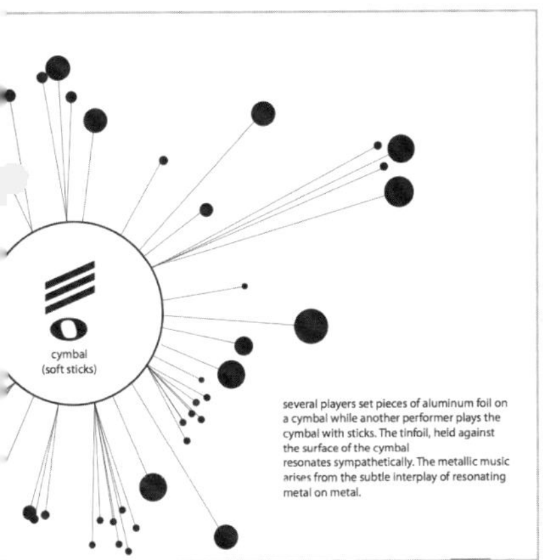

The narrative of *Auksalaq* incorporates fragmented and conflicting perspectives about the state of climate change as experienced in Alaska and the Arctic. These accounts, portrayed in the form of scientific commentary and interviews with people of the region, are woven into a story about change in the far north. The music expresses interlocking environmental forces as eco-musical forms, portraying the profound changes in the ice floes of Arctic waters. The media presents vivid imagery of Arctic land, sea, and sky, as well as scientific data and animation. An interactive audience-participation software called NOMADS enables engagement with the performance in real time across all the stages.

· · · · ·

One of Burtner's next projects will be to compose a large-scale piece with UVA professor and poet, Rita Dove. Like *Auksalaq,* the piece will be telematic and audience-interactive. It will use diffused performers and speakers to create a kind of musical-poetic garden. This piece has received a National Endowment for the Arts "Art Works" Grant.

Both Ms. Dove (see next page) and Mr. Burtner presented their work at the OpenGrounds launch in March 2012, where—in the spirit of OpenGrounds—they began their conversation about a future artistic collaboration.

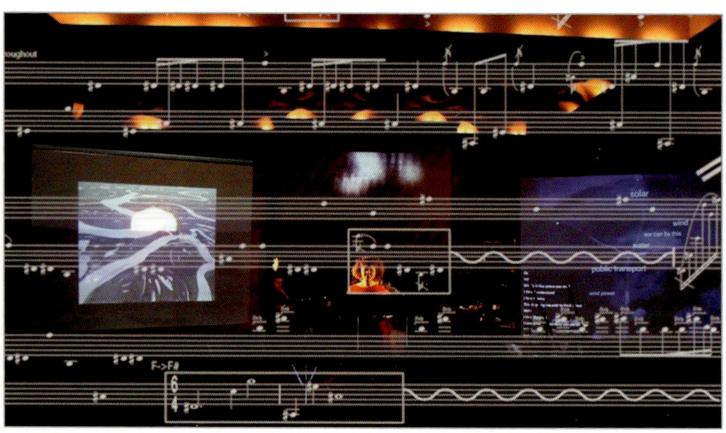

left

Detail of Matthew Burtner's score for *Auksalaq*
© Matthew Burtner, 2012, BMI

opposite

Details from *Auksalaq* performance and details of Matthew Burtner's score for*Auksalaq*
© Matthew Burtner, 2012, BMI

fade out
going som
sad

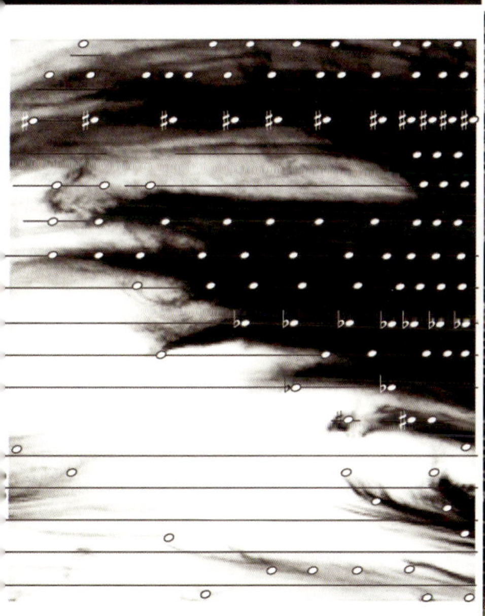

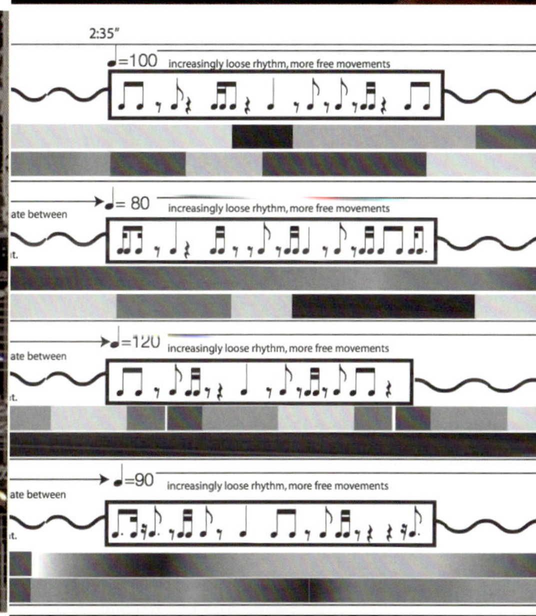
2:35"
=100 increasingly loose rhythm, more free movements
ate between
= 80 increasingly loose rhythm, more free movements
ate between
=120 increasingly loose rhythm, more free movements
ate between
=90 increasingly loose rhythm, more free movements

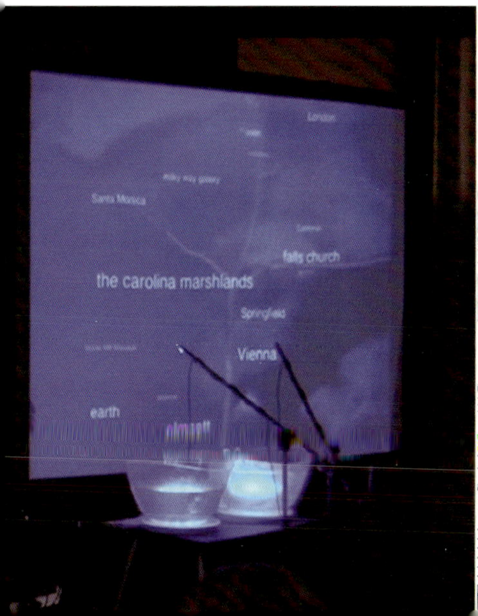
London
Santa Monica
falls church
the carolina marshlands
Springfield
Vienna
earth

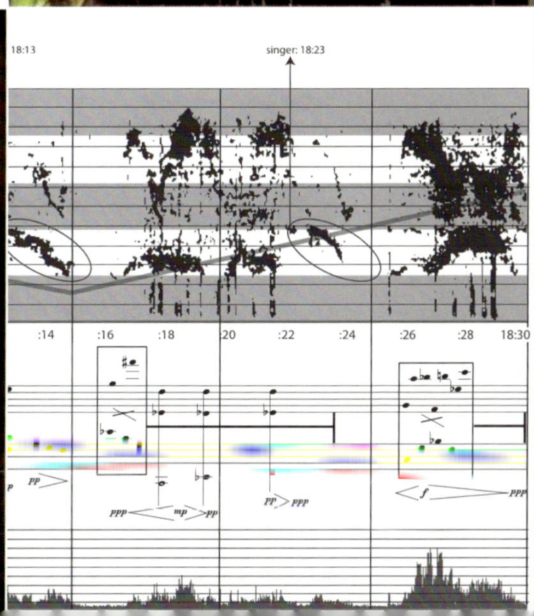
18:13
singer: 18:23
:14
:16
:18
:20
:22
:24
:26
:28
18:30

Rita Dove
openGROUNDS

Geometry

by

Rita Dove
former Poet Laureate
of the United States
and Commonwealth Professor
University of Virginia

I prove a theorem and the house expands:
the windows jerk free to hover near the ceiling,
the ceiling floats away with a sigh.

As the walls clear themselves of everything
but transparency, the scent of carnations
leaves with them. I am out in the open

And above the windows have hinged into butterflies,
sunlight glinting where they've intersected.
They are going to some point true and unproven.

This poem was read by Rita Dove at the OpenGrounds inaugural event, March 2012.

As is only fitting for our context at Thomas Jefferson's university, design is critical to the mission of OpenGrounds. From the "palette"—name, space, color, mark—to the "platform"—tables, walls, and grid—each element has been carefully crafted to support boundary-crossing, culture-changing "practice." Conceived by a community of designers, these elements recognize history while setting a trajectory into the 21st century.

Palette . Platform . Practice

Design

. seek . explore . question . **link** . laugh . change . impact. challenge . dream . risk . respect . engage .

. interact . **open** . hope . cross . studio . **connect** . prototype . laboratory .

. share . garage . **collaborate** . design . experiment . transgresss . test. **learn** . partner . innovate . make .

. inspire . **lead** . translate . cooperate . **grounds**

. expand . bridge . support . initiate . design . build . invent . **create** . accelerate . network . system .

. pursue . produce . craft . catalyze . **live** . discover . realize . understand . inquire . imagine . transform .

connect . collaborate . create | uva

Palette

Name

Open – both an adjective and a verb signifying a capacity to receive the unknown, to face the future without fear, to connect without reservation

Grounds – Thomas Jefferson's name for the University of Virginia campus, more than a surface or domain but inclusive of the soil and plants, the geological strata and the human designs, the inherited and constructed foundation of human civilization and the record of its values

. . . . .

As words joined in a fraught union, OpenGrounds describes both a new university addressing the urgent challenges of the future and the revolutionary origins of the University of Virginia, a community built around a shared public ground, anchored at one end by a pantheon of human knowledge, open at the other to unknown possibilities. That diagram still holds force in the 21st century as a platform for the programs and interactions from which the ideas for leadership will spring. The name implies the need for innovation, for an entrepreneurial spirit, for shared work with diverse partners, for creative engagement, and for the distillation of experience to provide an ethical foothold in the face of uncertainty.

The name OpenGrounds does not specify its institutional form, boundaries, or predetermined place in the structure of the academy. Its fluidity is its essence, allowing a nimble response to opportunity and the provision of interim support to launch new initiatives. OpenGrounds is a home for the curious and the collaborative; it has a starting point but no predetermined outcome or final form—it is an agent for the transformation of lives and institutions.

Palette

Space

by

William Sherman

architect

Human bonds are forged through shared experiences that detach from the background patterns of life to imprint themselves as a shared memory. This is the first task of architecture as a primary medium for the construction of a culture. The charge for the design of OpenGrounds was to imagine it as a place where one would know immediately that a different behavior would be expected, where the context would be sufficiently unfamiliar that a new set of rules would come into play. Unlike other spaces of the university—the seminar room, lecture hall, study carrel, or lounge—the expected behavior would be unspecified here, with a new culture being catalyzed by the character of the space. Originally housing the University Bookstore in the "Entrance Building" joining the city to the university, the space acknowledges its origins as a commercial loft, updated to connect globally through state-of-the-art technology. The dialogue between the contemporary and the archaic, the digital and the physical, pervades the space—the rolling concrete jigsaw-puzzle tables require a collaborative physical commitment to arrange; the 18-inch-thick masonry whiteboard walls evoke a visceral sense of cave painting while the 21st-century connectivity is housed in industrial aluminum chair rails. Main Street to the north and the passing sun to the south connect the space to the rhythms of the day. A full-day retreat here is the antithesis of those in windowless conference-center meeting rooms. Students and faculty share the common ground on equal terms as classes reinvent their patterns and collaborators fabricate prototypes or Skype with Norwegian poets.

openGROUNDS

Palette
Color

by
Anne Chesnut
graphic designer

After examination of a number of potential color combinations, two were selected for their simple associations: green for "grounds" in reference to earth and grass, and blue for "open" in reference to the sky, air, and endless space. Pairings of varying hues, intensities, and values of blue and green and their relationship to each other were scrutinized (right). From these possibilities, the final set was chosen (below) to support the concept of OpenGrounds because the blue and green are visual equals, neither more dominant than the other, and they appear substantial on a white field.

The complete color palette (left) consists of the OpenGrounds blue and green plus the university's orange and blue, which are used sparingly for emphasis or to call attention to details. Three shades of grey serve as neutrals. The palette has been applied, either in part or in full, to all digital and print pieces, further endowing OpenGrounds communications with a consistent presentation and helping to firmly establish its identity.

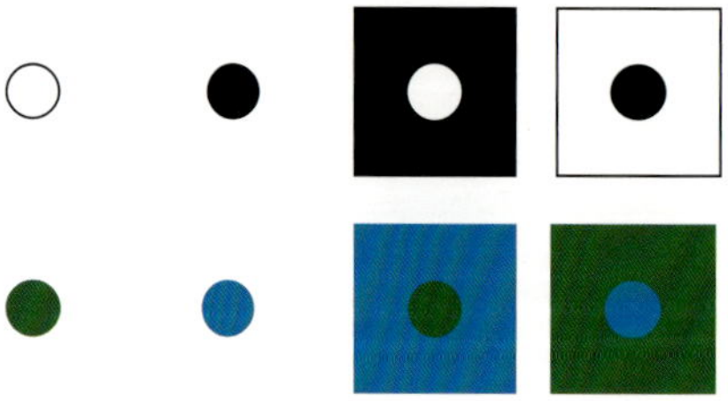

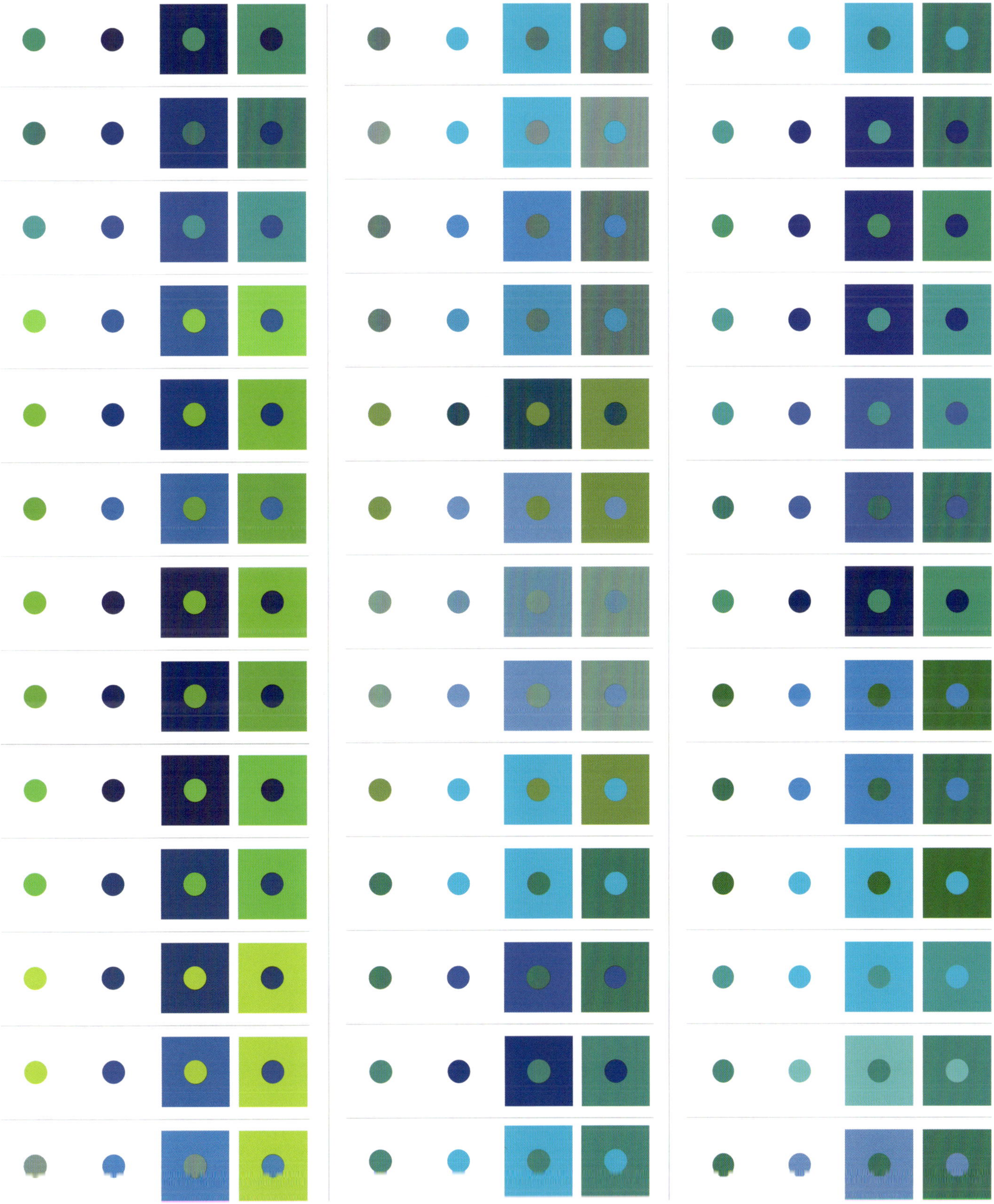

a descender and an ascender

The second and second-to-last letters, the descending p and ascending d, provide an asymmetrical balance, like bookends, to either end of the logotype.

unconnected bowls

As a subtle visual reference to "open," the second letters of open and grounds, the p and R, have been altered so that the initial vertical stroke no longer fully connects to the curved bowl.

By design, the strokes on e and d remain connected.

mixed alphabets

Blending lower- and uppercases with ambiguous letters benefits the mark.

Without spacing, the second word's start is signaled by color and by the switch to an uppercase G following the all-lowercase "open." Use of G avoids the elaborate lowercase form, making for more uniform lettering throughout. Mixing small caps, G R N, with characters that could be either case, O U S, permits a lowercase d to be introduced to "grounds" while further distinguishing it from "open."

color balance

The intensities and values of the designated colors give the two words equal importance despite extreme discrepancy in length.

Palette

Mark

by

Anne Chesnut

graphic designer

The mark, developed during the ideological gestation period, was OpenGrounds' first tangible form, since it preceded the Corner Studio's completed renovation. The logotype's structure was informed by the vision of OpenGrounds as an exploratory, risk-taking place as well as a neutral space for partnership. With the opening of the Corner Studio, the mark continues to play an important supportive role in promoting awareness of OpenGrounds and its values beyond the physical location.

OpenGrounds can be viewed as a double portal by virtue of both location and principle—an entry *to* the university for external communities and a pathway *to* the world from academia. Accordingly, the mark bridges the two without becoming a subset of the university's brand. In deference to external communities, the popular colloquial name, UVA, was embraced as part of the tagline (though formal publications, such as this, also utilize the university logo).

Rather than base the logo on a face with 18th century typographic idiosyncrasies, the selection of a typeface from which to redraw letters to create a logotype was made through careful examination of multiple contemporary faces. Considerations included associated weights for the mark and potential for display and editorial copy. Whitney, a sans serif typeface originally designed for the Whitney Museum by Tobias Frere-Jones, ultimately became the point of departure for the logotype's drawing and was adopted as the typeface for ephemeral communications and enduring publications, like OpenGrounds' first forum book: *Changing Views: Photography and Environmental Action.*

openGROUNDS

connect. collaborate. create | uva

tagline

The dual tagline suggests both the possibilities and potential of OpenGrounds as an innovative space for new initiatives and the university as host of a shared place for engagement between academia and local and global communities.

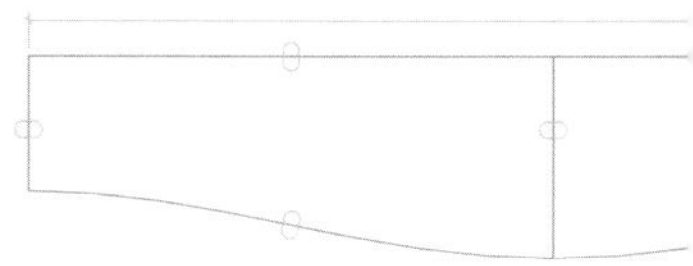

Platform

Table Configurations

by

William Sherman
architect
Alexander Kitchin
concrete designer and fabricator

The tables are the product of a collaboration with Alexander Kitchin, a faculty member and skilled concrete fabricator, upending expectations of convenience promoted by commercial vendors of furniture for collaboration. The tables are designed for connection rather than convenience—the experience of working together to move them into place is a time of shared enterprise. The jigsaw puzzle-like shapes create a variety of spatial structures for collaboration, from individual spaces with laptops docked against the walls, to ovals, rectangles, or curving lines. Each table has the substance and character to be a meeting place or a stage. The surface itself, a striped hybrid of stock aluminum grating and black concrete, invites curiosity and surprise. When in their docked position, the tables form counters for individuals, piers for two or three, or lobes for groups of five or six, or serving counters or pedestals, while leaving the floor open for a range of possible activities. A table is a second ground, elevated to connect bodies in space, establishing or countering hierarchies, enabling conversation.

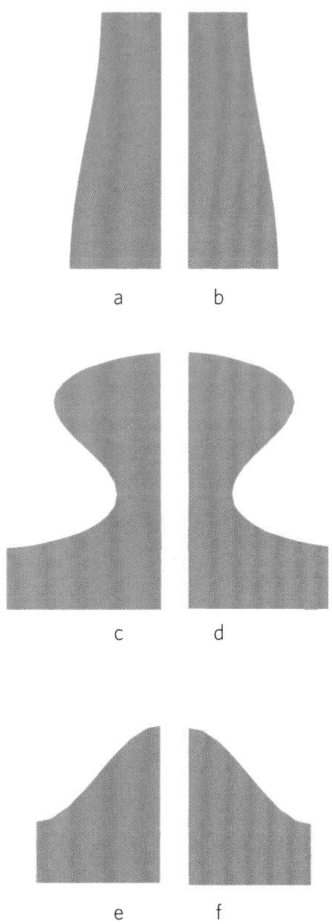

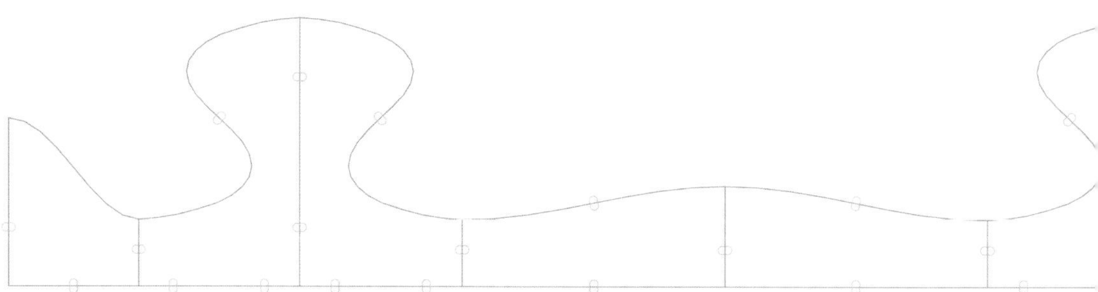

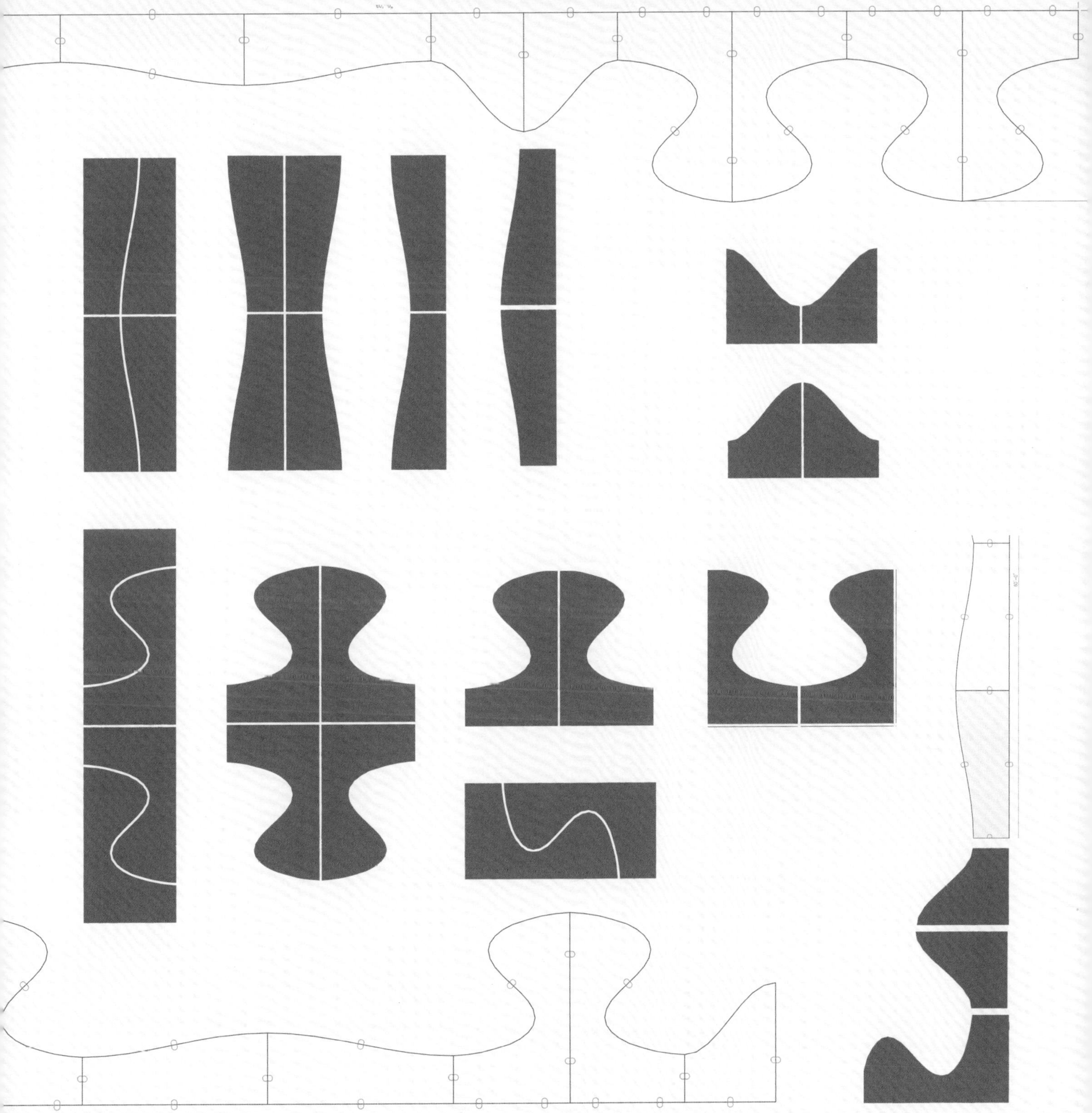

Platform

The Walls: Whiteboards and Rails

by

William Sherman
architect
Roger Sherry
designer and fabricator

For at least 30,000 years, humans have been writing and drawing on walls, marking and sharing their observations and insights. At OpenGrounds, this most ancient and user-friendly technology is combined with the most advanced, to create the maxiumum spectrum of ways to move ideas that percolate in the mind out into the world to be shared and cultivated. The original walls at OpenGrounds, solid masses of brick and plaster, have all been activated as communication media for writing, projecting, using touchscreens, and poster hanging. Rails fabricated from standard aluminum channels contain wiring and access for communication and power, while also forming a dock for the tables and a shelf for books recommended by faculty and friends. The new steel framework walls containing the needed services for the space are clad in removable panels, which create a site for experimentation as engineering and architecture students design prototypes of active interfaces. Beyond the visual communication, faculty from the music and drama departments have designed a sound system as suited for digital experimentation and laptop orchestras as it is for the human voice sharing stories from African communities. With a disciplined design integration to put the content in the foreground, the walls of OpenGrounds form an invitation to create and collaborate, to transform the space each day, limited only by the imagination.

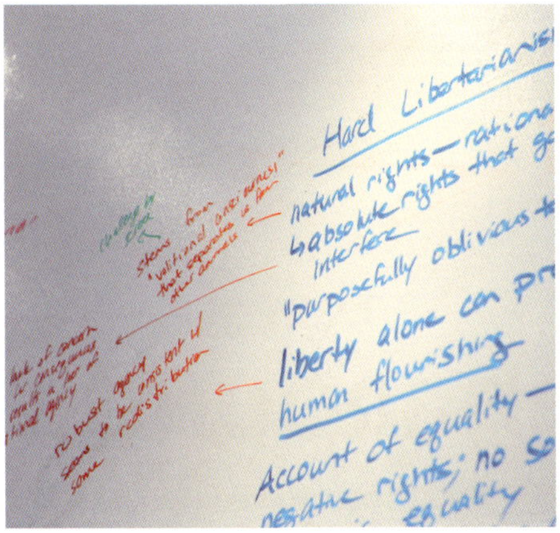

openGROUNDs

connect. collaborate. create | UVA

Platform
The Grid

by
Anne Chesnut
graphic designer
William Sherman
architect

Like the other components of the OpenGrounds platform intended to encourage connection and exchange, lower barriers, and inspire interaction, the use of a grid as defining graphic element for OpenGrounds was a carefully calculated motif. Unlike the more common graph or linear grid featuring closed squares, the dot grid is an unbounded open network.

Used by OpenGrounds for both its print and web communications, the dot grid has a historic resonance as its use was partially inspired by Thomas Jefferson's diagram for the nation's capital (below). Jefferson's dots indicate the unknown future for areas beyond Georgetown and Rock Creek and south of the Capitol. The dot grid application on notepads (opposite), which can be found scattered throughout the Corner Studio for participant use, also conveys a sense of unknown potential through the myriad possible dot-to-dot connections or simply as a way to align written notes.

On printed publications, like the OpenGrounds brochure (sample spread shown below), the grid can be seen to intersect, tie together, or determine placement for both text and images. As graphic detail, it symbolically references many of the concepts associated with OpenGrounds, including openness, alternative pathways, possible intersections, and reinventable spaces.

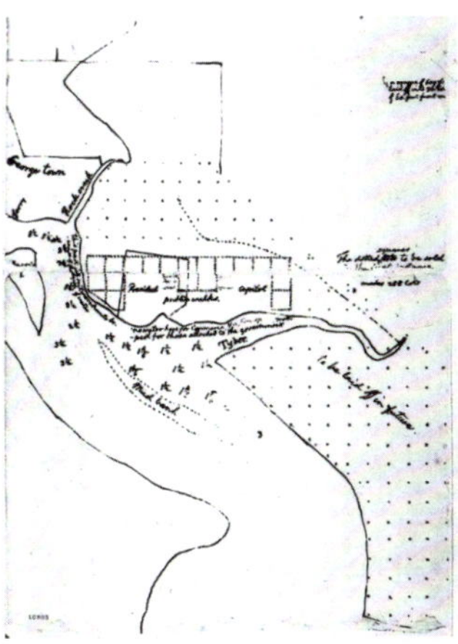

Practice

Posters

by

Anne Chesnut

graphic designer

A unified identity is presented in OpenGrounds communications regardless of format, use, size, or quantity through the consistent application of elements from its palette and platform. Color selection is primarily based on the OpenGrounds palette and all copy appears in the typeface associated with the mark. The dot grid is frequently employed to embody the page with an added sense of structure.

The vertical orientation of the OpenGrounds logotype and accompanying tagline on printed materials, from large banners to small fliers, serves several purposes including resolving spatial issues. The placement does not solely establish identity but re-proportions the page to a more desirable shape; emerging from a squat 5.5x8.5 program, 8.5x11 flier, or 11x17 poster, the primary content area is reformatted to a more elegant elongated rectangle. Taking advantage of the longer dimension increases the mark's size, which also facilitates the recognition of a new entity.

HEARST *business media*

UNIVERSITY *of* VIRGINIA

openGROUNDS

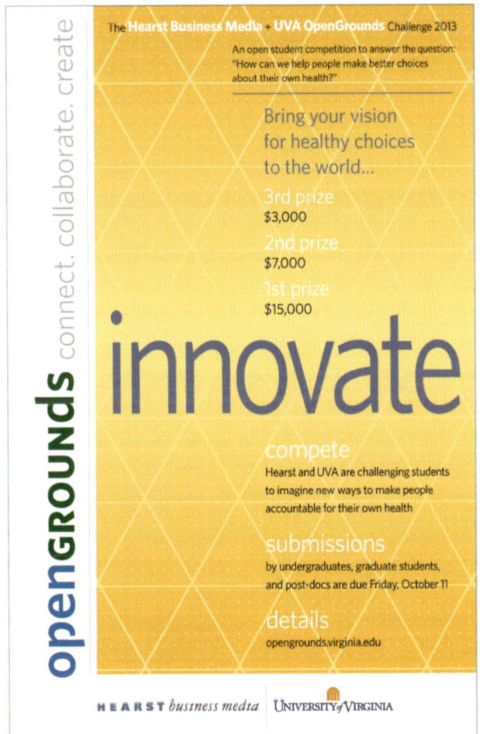

four-piece series

To introduce new programming, like the challenges with Vonage and Hearst, and to promote these opportunities to a broad audience, OpenGrounds opted for sequential campaign materials

Each of the serial posters advances an aspect of a challenge while also communicating the basic pertinent information so they could be hung consecutively or individually.

component parts

The Hearst building's dominant architectural element, the triangle, was translated into a triangular grid, which was integrated with the OpenGrounds dot grid to create a universal field for the poster series promoting the joint challenge.

A color from the Hearst mark and another from OpenGrounds' palette created the two-color scheme.

The vertical application of the OpenGrounds mark is consistent with its use on other printed pieces and determined the placement of two additional, incongruous marks, for Hearst Business Media and UVA, in a supportive role.

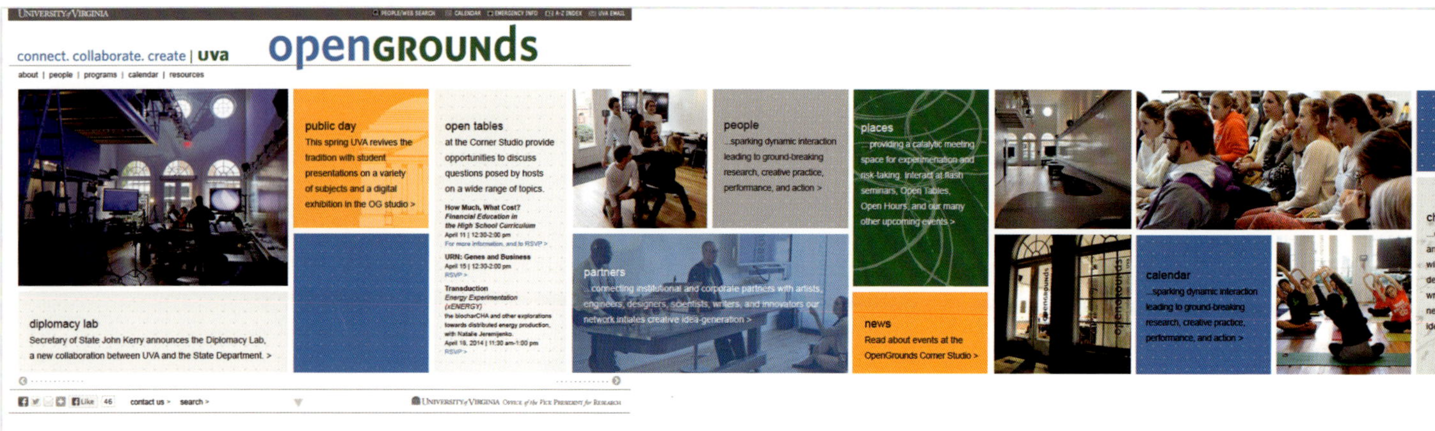
connect. collaborate. create | uva
openGROUNDS
about | people | programs | calendar | resources
public day
This spring UVA revives the tradition with student presentations on a variety of subjects and a digital exhibition in the OG studio >
open tables
at the Corner Studio provide opportunities to discuss questions posed by hosts on a wide range of topics.
people
...sparking dynamic interaction leading to ground-breaking research, creative practice, performance, and action >
places
...providing a catalytic meeting space for experimentation and risk-taking. Interact at flash seminars, Open Tables, Open Hours, and our many other upcoming events >
diplomacy lab
Secretary of State John Kerry announces the Diplomacy Lab, a new collaboration between UVA and the State Department >
partners
...connecting institutional and corporate partners with artists, engineers, designers, scientists, writers, and innovators our network initiates creative idea-generation >
news
Read about events at the OpenGrounds Corner Studio >
calendar
...sparking dynamic interaction leading to ground-breaking research, creative practice, performance, and action >
contact us >
search >

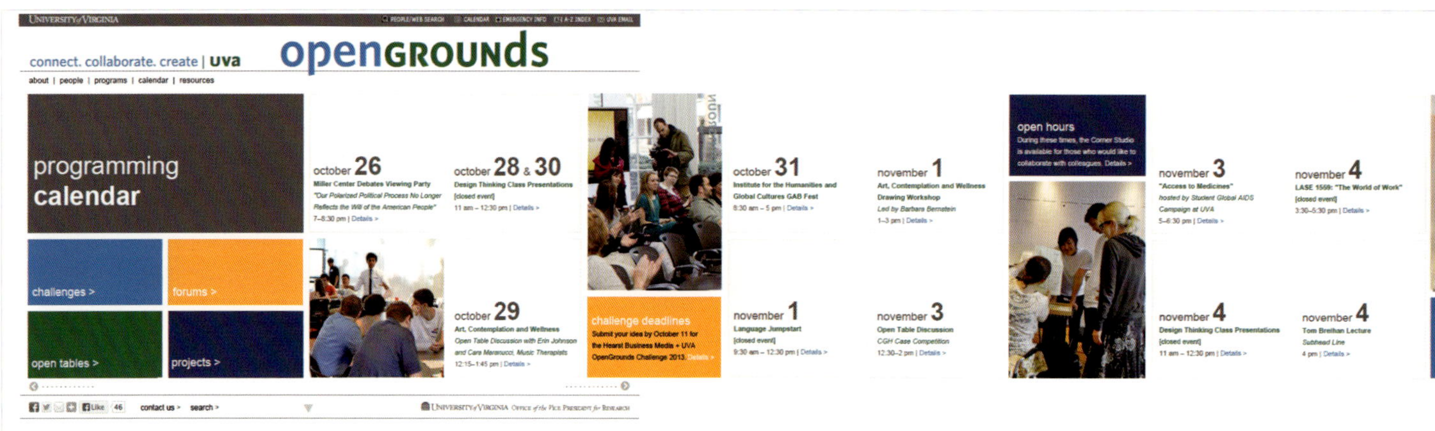
connect. collaborate. create | uva
openGROUNDS
about | people | programs | calendar | resources
programming calendar
challenges >
forums >
open tables >
projects >
october 26
october 28 & 30
october 31
november 1
november 3
november 4
november 4
october 29
challenge deadlines
november 1
november 3
november 4
november 4
open hours
contact us >
search >

Practice

Web

by

Anne Chesnut

graphic designer

The site, now in its second generation, has moved beyond just promoting a new exploratory space and its potential for collaboration and innovation. It now not only publicizes opportunities for engagement but examines what has transpired during OpenGrounds' first two and a half years of programming.

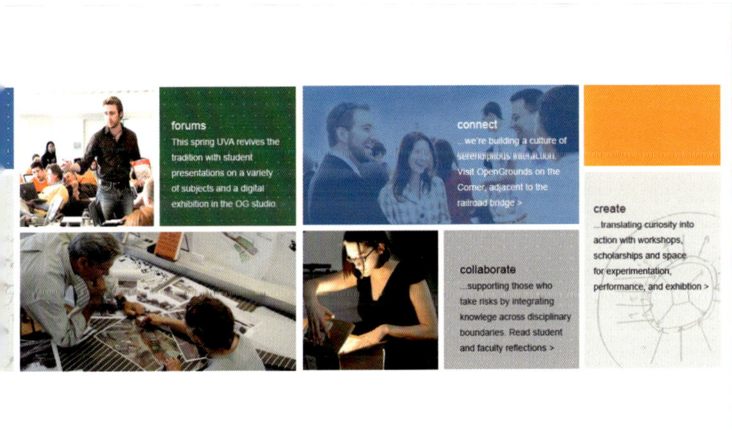

Both versions of the site, the introductory one and the newly redesigned one, have not used the ubiquitous vertical scroll with its implied hierarchy of information from top to bottom. Rather than adopting what was expected or easiest to implement, we arranged images and text to slide horizontally across the screen. This was not a decision to go against the dominant convention but rather a considered choice concerning function and viewing opportunities. The sideways orientation readily supports aspects of responsive design, such as video format and the tendency to read in landscape orientation on smaller devices like smart phones. Further, as a showcase, the horizontal orientation offers numerous presentation styles for program stories. Moving laterally can be reminiscent of turning book pages, evoke a portfolio viewing, or be akin to walking through a physical space.

Application of the OpenGrounds color palette and graphic element, the dot grid, on the website ensures continuity and a consistent identity with printed publications.

Practice

Adaptability

Perhaps the greatest factor contributing to the success of OpenGrounds is its adaptability. Not merely because it enables us to reconfigure the space in seemingly endless variations, but, importantly, because this adaptability allows us to say "yes!" and allows our partners to feel a deeper sense of ownership and investment.

OpenGrounds staff and interns must be prepared to respond nimbly in every situation. When a potential partner approaches us with an idea for a project or event, we can meet almost any request, and we can jointly imagine the expanded possibilities of what the event could be. From moving the tables and writing on the whiteboards to utilizing the projection wall or audio system, the space is designed for daily transformation—and we relish the opportunity to try something new. By embodying the ideals of a space that is not fixed, but constantly in the process of being made, we invite our visitors into a creative process of place making.

As we work collaboratively to remake the space, OpenGrounds is working to shift behaviors, to open partners to new ways of working together and new ways of inhabiting a space through active participation rather than passive occupation. OpenGrounds has been designed as an open system that invites, and indeed demands, engagement. The space offers a two-way dialogue through which partners imagine and explore new possibilities, shifting their behaviors in the process. By participating in the adaptation of the space, partners feel invested, connected to the work in a new way.

THE PENGUIN ANTHOLOGY OF 20TH CENTURY AMERICAN POETRY

clouds

OpenGrounds
Where Imagination Becomes Real

by

Tom Skalak
Vice President for Research

> "Everything you can imagine is real."
> — Pablo Picasso

OpenGrounds was imagined as a new way of life for the University of Virginia and our worldwide partners. After two years of existence, OpenGrounds is real. In the eyes of OpenGrounds, collisions among the disciplines and creative partners from all walks of life are inevitable. OpenGrounds accelerates them and celebrates them. OpenGrounds offers a spiritual home for ideation and collaboration, with the goal of meaningful expression, action, and impact that make a positive difference in the world. OpenGrounds offers the courage to explore when it is needed, and applauds the courageous who design their own journeys. It is a "chapel" where the feeling is instilled (for all disciplines and boundaries that have settled into place over time) that one can leave for the destination of one's own imagination.

> "A boundary is not that at which something stops but, as the Greeks recognized, the boundary is that from which something *begins its presencing*."
> — Martin Heidegger

The origin and growth of OpenGrounds were not a given at the start. We owe thanks to many people who supported the idea of OpenGrounds from an early stage. John Abele, founding chairman of Boston Scientific Corporation and widely known as the philosopher-king of that continuous-learning organization during its remarkable growth years, provided substantial input and guidance to offer a "palette of collaboration" that would open the doors of OpenGrounds to a diverse array of partners, including adversaries and friends, experts and novices, professionals and students of all ages. John enthusiastically urged us to "challenge existing methods" and to seek the collective wisdom of networks extending far beyond the academic grounds. Dorothy Kosinski, director of The Phillips Collection in Washington, D.C., partnered with us from early stages, based on our shared belief that the intersection of fields including art, science, technology, media, and others could produce radical and useful advances, broaden appreciation for world-class art collections, and attract talent. We deeply appreciate Dorothy's courage to seize upon a set of ideas and take risks to pursue them with us enthusiastically.

Rich Malloch, president of Hearst Business Media, based in Manhattan, was an early supporter of OpenGrounds programs as well. In placing great value on curiosity and creativity among his national executive team, Rich was able to help us design and implement several OpenGrounds workshops and challenges involving Hearst executives, UVA students and faculty, and other partners. We greatly appreciate his recognition that by seeing the world clearly, with curiosity about its continuing changes, an individual or an organization (whether corporate, non-governmental, educational, or other) can best adapt and thrive in a changing world. OpenGrounds provides a platform for exactly this sort of continuous observation, ideation, and learning. Marc Lefar, CEO of Vonage, an international telecommunications company, has been a committed champion of OpenGrounds challenges, related research into the nature of virality, and the UVA Entrepreneurship Cup competition, a Grounds-wide event that has inspired hundreds of UVA students to develop their most creative concepts. We have appreciated the personal insight based on deep design and innovation experiences that Marc has offered to OpenGrounds participants. Cheryl Wagner, chief of staff in our Office of the Vice President for Research, was essential in the early days of the OpenGrounds programming, helping to bring the ideal mix of people and concepts together in just the right atmosphere. Teresa Sullivan, president of the University of Virginia, saw the value of OpenGrounds from the beginning and took the leadership steps to make the ideas and programs a part of the Cornerstone Plan, highly visible, and available to the entire university community. We are grateful for Terry's support at every step of the development, from involving diverse alumni by integrating the OpenGrounds concept into the President's Box at major football games, to the launch event, to today's physical studio spaces that accommodate the exponentially increasing student and faculty demands for OpenGrounds engagement.

> "Life isn't about finding yourself.
> Life is about creating yourself."
>
> — **George Bernard Shaw**

As UVA student Ben DiNapoli puts it: "I think of OpenGrounds as an opportunity for students... exploring creative paths." Nick Lee, Class of 2015, said, "OpenGrounds is an irreplaceable catalyst in fostering new student leaders..."—an essential element of UVA's commitment to our students' personal growth in the Cornerstone Plan. Another student said, "The most valuable aspect of my experience at OpenGrounds has definitely been my exposure to the optimistic, progressive mindset the place seems to promote." It is gratifying indeed to see the impact of the OpenGrounds experience on UVA student life and students' growth as creative, collaborative leaders.

We were honored to host Peter Schjeldahl, the chief art critic of *The New Yorker* magazine, at an OpenGrounds gathering assembled in the pursuit of "art-science collaborations" at The Phillips Collection. He advised us that he had long reflected on the professional separations we tend to accept, on occasion telling painters, "You paint, I'll write." Peter read from a paperback copy of the collected poems of Wallace Stevens, which he had acquired earlier in the day by walking down the street from The Phillips Collection in Washington, D.C., to a local bookstore, after imagining what he would say to our group. Standing in a gallery room, in the presence of world masterpieces of visual art including paintings by Matisse and van Gogh, he read the Stevens poem "The Idea of Order at Key West," painting a picture of "...The lights in the fishing boats at anchor there,/As the night descended, tilting in the air, ..." It was a moving performance. Peter provided a superb role model for the close OpenGrounds integration of the "creative" and "analytical," as the printed words, so carefully chosen by the poet and then read aloud so simply, inspired the people gathered there as deeply as the eternal works of art surrounding them.

The structure of this book, *Link . Learn . Lead . Live,* is well illustrated by the many examples provided. Of the four L's, I want to concentrate on the significance of the last one—Live. It prompts us to ask: Live in what way? This question is at the heart of OpenGrounds. It is a way of living, a way of behaving, a way of interacting that opens new possibilities to our vision. At the launch event for OpenGrounds, this concept was beautifully illustrated by Philippe Cousteau, CNN's global environmental correspondent and an ecosystems activist. Philippe told of a remote African village that depended for its subsistence on fish caught in the local river, from brackish and sometimes dangerous waters. His team placed a number of the fish into a holding tank, and provided snorkeling masks to the local fishermen—proud tribesmen between 20 and 40 years of age—who had never before seen the fish swimming in their natural environment. They were amazed and delighted to see the graceful motions of the fish as they swam underwater, full of life. They depended upon them, yet had never seen them alive. What a wonderful example this offered for OpenGrounds—to be aware of and appreciate the special things that are often right beside us. This is a key to authentic collaborations—those that are rooted in deep appreciation, passion, and integrity.

To create new and lasting elements of culture requires vision and leadership. I would like to recognize and thank Bill Sherman, the founding director, for his invaluable leadership, which has set the character of authentic collaboration for OpenGrounds. Bill is not only the founder of OpenGrounds, an award-winning architect, and a dedicated professor of architecture—he is also the designer of the OpenGrounds space, furnishings, media, technology, and programs. His unique background blends an acute sense of the arts and humanities over human history with practical experience in design, technology development, and the professions as ways to engage with the world and produce tangible actions that matter. Bill's gift of this unique experience has allowed OpenGrounds to come alive. His appreciation for the creative spirit within all disciplines, his innate collaborative sensibility, his feeling for the primacy of human relationships in great accomplishments, and his can-do maker skills have all been essential. I remember seeing Bill and his wife, Nicole, working in tandem over a weekend to put the finishing touches on the OpenGrounds studio for the launch. Bill was guiding the assembly of the modular whiteboard wall sections, and Nicole, an accomplished jewelry designer in her own right, was power-sanding the unique OpenGrounds concrete and metal tables (symbolizing the union of dissimilar materials and ideas) to a precision finish. One has only to scan his own writing to see the intellectual verve he's brought to this effort. Bill observes that people share this new common ground to "fabricate prototypes" or to "Skype with Norwegian poets," that "fluidity is its essence," and that "for at least 30,000 years, humans have been writing and drawing on walls." Bill can imagine the future, and he can make it happen. This is an uncommon collection of knowledge and skills in a single individual, and we've been fortunate to enjoy Bill's leadership and inspiration as OpenGrounds' founding director. Lindsey Hepler, associate director, complements Bill's role on the OpenGrounds leadership team, bringing her background in the performing arts and dance to the programs. Lindsey has been instrumental in sparking new relationships among the diverse people who frequent OpenGrounds, leading to new programs and higher levels of community and student engagement. She brings special life and comprehensive understanding to the OpenGrounds environment, elevating our aspirations.

> "To live is the rarest thing in the world.
> Most people exist, that is all."
>
> — Oscar Wilde

OpenGrounds offers to all a rare, yet enduring, way to live. Our greatest hope is that future generations of students, faculty, partners, and professionals will seek out this "rarest thing in the world"—and move through OpenGrounds to the journeys of their own imaginations.

Acknowledgements

This publication has come together thanks to our partners and collaborators within and beyond the University of Virginia who have taken the time to work with and through OpenGrounds in the past two and a half years. We are deeply grateful to all who have helped make these first two and a half years such a success.

We must begin by expressing our gratitude to Tom Skalak and Teresa Sullivan, who have been the champions of OpenGrounds from initial idea, through concept development, implementation, and in 2015, expansion. Thank you for your visionary leadership and unending support.

We are deeply thankful for the essential early guidance and advice from John Abele, Chic Thompson, Jaffray Woodriff, Philippe Cousteau and Andrew Snowhite. These visionary thinkers brought their experience, networks of relationships in diverse fields, and personal energy to the initial vision for OpenGrounds.

We extend our gratitude to Cheryl Wagner, who has played a crucial role with OpenGrounds from the start, offering her extraordinary support in getting OpenGrounds up and running. We would also like to recognize Michael Rasbury and Matthew Burtner for their early involvement in imagining the space, for continuing to push the boundaries of what we think is possible, and for populating OpenGrounds with hundreds of artists and musicians.

For their essential role in the completion of this publication, we thank our fabulous graphic designer and true collaborator, Anne Chesnut; and our skillful copy editor, Margo Browning.

We extend a huge thank you to our partners beyond the University of Virginia who have made our programs and this publication possible: Chic Thompson, our continued collaborator and brainstorming partner who keeps us smiling; Dorothy Kosinski and Klaus Ottmann at The Phillips Collection; Marc Lefar and JoAnn Tizzano at Vonage; Rich Malloch at Hearst Business Media; and Tomicah Tilleman and Zack Haas, our Diplomacy Lab partners at the State Department. Within the University of Virginia, we are so fortunate to have the opportunity to work with such incredible faculty and staff collaborators: Rebecca Dillingham, April Ballard, and Colleen Laurence, our wonderful neighbors in the Center for Global Health; Stewart Gamage, Director of Morven Programs, our great friend and Diplomacy Lab co-conspirator; Michael Levenson, Keicy Tolbert, and Angela Nemecek with the Institute of the Humanities and Global Cultures; Cassandra Fraser, Professor of Chemistry (and so much more), the leader of the Transduction project; Willis Jenkins, Associate Professor of Religion, Ethics, and Environment, and instigator of conversations about Environmental Humanities; Jon Bellona, Rachel Vassar, Gwendolyn McGinn, and Erik Deluca, our incredibly talented Art and Environmental Action Student Scholars. Lastly, we are deeply indebted to the many students who have worked with us from the start. We could not do what we do without the energy and enthusiasm of the students, particularly our incredible team of interns—thank you! —WS, LH

OpenGrounds, University of Virginia
PO Box 800317
Charlottesville VA 22908-0317
opengrounds.virginia.edu

ISBN 978- 0-9893995-1-7

Colophon

Designer
Anne Chesnut
Charlottesville VA

Managing editor
Lindsey Hepler
Charlottesville VA

Copy editor
Margo Browning
Charlottesville VA

Photographers
Dan Addison/UVA University Communications
Erica Ruth, Class of 2015
John J. Park
Andrew Precious, Class of 2016
William Sherman
Tom Daly

Printer
Worth Higgins & Associates, Inc.
Richmond VA

Stock
McCoy Silk Text & Cover

Type
Whitney